No. 1

Commerce with **Conscience?**

Human Rights and
Corporate Codes
of Conduct

Related Publications of the Centre

Occasional Papers

*The Relationship between Trade and Rights in the
Context of Foreign Policy* by Ed Broadbent - 1996

*Globalization and Workers' Human Rights
in the APEC Region* by Diana Bronson and
Stéphanie Rousseau - 1996

*Globalization, Trade and Human Rights: The
Canadian Business Perspective: A Summary Report
of the Toronto Confe*rence - 1996

Essay Series

*Human Rights, Labour Standards and the New World
Trade Organization: Opportunities for a Linkage*
by Christine Elwell - 1995

ISBN 2-922084-07-8

*Legal Deposit:
Bibliothèque nationale du Québec, 2nd quarter, 1997
National Library of Canada, 2nd quarter, 1997*

*Printed in Canada
Design: François Blais design graphique
Proofreading: William Mersereau*

*International Centre for Human Rights
and Democratic Development
63, rue de Brésoles
Montréal (Québec)
Canada H2Y 1V7*

No. 1

Commerce with **Conscience?**

Human Rights and
Business Codes
of Conduct

by CRAIG FORCESE

Canadian Lawyers Association for
International Human Rights (CLAIHR)
in collaboration with the International
Centre for Human Rights and
Democratic Development

INTERNATIONAL CENTRE FOR HUMAN RIGHTS
AND DEMOCRATIC DEVELOPMENT

TABLE OF CONTENTS

ACKNOWLEDGEMENTS

I gratefully acknowledge the contribution of Monica Lambton who demonstrated incredible diligence and professionalism in overseeing the study's business survey phase. Much credit for the findings of this report go to her. Further thanks go to the Canadian Lawyers Association for International Human Rights (CLAIHR) volunteer research team: Peter Copeland, Ella Heyder, Kim Inksater, Allan McChesney, Darryl Robinson. I would also like to thank the numerous members of the non-profit and business communities who participated in the project. Aaron Freeman of *Multinational Monitor* deserves special thanks for his careful editing and comments, as do Stéphanie Rousseau and Diana Bronson of ICHRDD. Richard Nadeau, Moira Hutchinson, Ann Weston and Philippe Spicher also provided critical insights. CLAIHR's office staff at the time of the study (volunteer and otherwise) also deserves special mention: Hector Cabrera, Al Cook, Isabelle Helal, Carolyn Rowe and Debrah Taylor. It goes without saying that while all these people made important contributions to the study, any errors or omissions are my own responsibility. Further, the conclusions reached in this report are my own and CLAIHR's, and not necessarily those of the people who made volunteer contributions to the project.

CRAIG FORCESE

Consumer goods from around the world, including many made in countries that systematically violate human rights, are now available in Canadian stores. In the mutual fund market, more and more Canadians are attracted to international growth funds. This situation raises questions about the responsibilities of Canadian corporations operating overseas as they relate to international human rights.

I am proud as President of the International Centre for Human Rights and Democratic Development (ICHRDD) to launch this study. The information included here should act as a wake-up call to corporations and consumers alike. Readers will quickly discover that corporations — and consumers — must do much more if the promise that globalization will lead to more rights and democracy is ever to ring true. The systematic violation of fundamental human rights, and in particular the rights of workers, presents a severe threat to the long-term viability of the global market place and to the peaceful and democratic development of societies where people share in the wealth that is generated by the much-touted globalization process.

In February 1996, the ICHRDD, in collaboration with the Business Council on National Issues, organized a conference entitled "Globalization, Trade and Human Rights: The Canadian Business Perspective." The discussions held that day, as well as many other debates in Canada and abroad, revolved around the implications of doing business in countries where human rights and workers' rights are abused, and the responsibilities of corporations in such contexts. One thing that both the business people and human rights activists agreed upon was the importance of businesses developing and implementing codes of conduct for their own operations. It is no longer enough to say "When in Rome, do as the Romans do." The question is rather: Can companies who are responsible at home be irresponsible abroad? Or, can companies afford to ignore the human rights which governments violate, despite their international commitments to protect them?

This study flows from the discussions that were held that day. The ICHRDD helped define the parameters for this research on codes of conduct and we provided modest financial support for the project. The actual research was done by the Canadian Lawyers Association for International Human Rights (CLAIHR), under the determined and meticulous direction of Craig Forcese. Our two organizations wanted to better understand the theory and practice behind human rights-sensitive codes of conduct as a means for businesses to voluntarily abide by core labour rights and standards. We wanted to know if Canadian businesses were or were not actually doing something in this area. Starting from an analysis of the use of domestic codes of conduct, then looking at the US business experience in developing and implementing human rights-sensitive codes of conduct for overseas sourcing or investment, this study details the results of a unique survey of Canada's largest corporations doing business abroad. The results provide a portrait of codes of conduct in Canada, and more specifically of human rights-sensitive codes of conduct for international operations.

The ICHRDD is committed to contributing to essential policy debates on the linkage between trade liberalization and respect for universal human rights. I invite readers to consider carefully the material in this report, and more than that, to act by raising the issue of corporate responsibility in their own communities, workplaces and with the companies they choose to buy from or invest in. A second publication, to appear later this year, will address in more detail some of the policy options that are available to businesses, governments, investors and citizens acting individually or collectively.

We would be most interested in your feedback on this study and I hope you enjoy reading it as much as I did.

HON. WARREN ALLMAND, P.C., Q.C.
President ICHRDD

INTRODUCTION

International businesses are becoming increasingly important players on the world stage. Human rights activists are focussing their attention more and more on large corporations who are being called to account for the impact of their practices on international human rights. Human rights organizations such as Human Rights Watch in New York and the International Secretariat of Amnesty International have either actively promoted the use of human rights-sensitive codes of conduct by firms operating internationally or have expressed an interest in doing so. In the United States, groups such as the National Labor Committee Education Fund in Support of Worker and Human Rights in Central America have launched protest campaigns designed to oblige corporations to effectively implement their codes of conduct, particularly those relating to the treatment of workers in Export Processing Zones. A similar campaign focussing on Levi Strauss and Nike has been launched by the Canadian Organization for Development and Peace, a Canadian non-governmental organization.

Governments have also begun promoting voluntary codes of conduct for national businesses operating overseas. In the United States, the Clinton Administration has sought to defuse criticism of its failure to consider human rights concerns during its renewal of China's most favoured nation trading status by promoting, however softly, a voluntary code of conduct for US businesses overseas.[1] A number of Congressional bills that would encourage US businesses to adhere to human rights standards in international operations have been introduced in both the House of Representatives and the Senate in recent sessions of Congress.[2] Similarly, in 1994, the then-governing Labour Party of Australia called for a national voluntary code for Australian businesses operating in the South Pacific. In Canada, meanwhile, corporate human rights codes of conduct are beginning to generate interest among business and political leaders.[3]

Arising from the present preoccupation with corporate codes of conduct are concerns that a focus on such voluntary measures will take pressure off governments to work towards more systematic means of encouraging respect for international human rights, such as linkages between trade and human rights. Many critics of codes see them as largely ineffectual, unenforceable and ultimately counterproductive, in part because corporations treat codes as public relations measures rather than obligatory covenants. Supporters see codes as pragmatic means to effect real change in a world where governments are increasingly reluctant to impose mandatory measures. Ethical behaviour and adherence to, and promotion of, international human rights norms, some observers argue, is in the corporation's best interest as human rights abuses lead ultimately to unstable economic and business environments. The job of the human rights movement is to make business leaders see this and act accordingly.

The dilemma implicit in the use of corporate codes of conduct as means of promoting human rights is illustrated by the example of South Africa. In 1977, the Reverend Leon Sullivan, a member of the General Motors board of directors, proposed the Sullivan Principles dealing with the behaviour of US corporations in South Africa. The Principles outlined a code of conduct designed to allow US corporations to operate in South Africa without partaking in the systematic human rights abuses characteristic of the apartheid regime. Many observers feel that firms generally did a good job abiding by the Principles.[4] Still, others note that corporations could not operate in South Africa without implicitly benefiting from a system whose economic purpose was the maintenance of cheap labour and without bolstering the staying power of the apartheid regime.[5] The success of the code stemmed not so much from the altruism or social responsibility of the corporations as from the realization that the alternative to the code was full-scale economic sanctions. Corporations were also motivated by potent shareholder pressure from large public pension funds and constraints imposed by US state and municipal governments on procurement from businesses operating in South Africa. In the absence of these "big sticks," adherence to the Principles may well have been less marked.[6]

This conclusion echoes findings from studies on Canadian domestic voluntary codes: "[t]ypically voluntary codes are a response to real or perceived threats: of a new law or regulation; of competitive pressures or trade sanctions; or of consumer pressures or boycotts."[7] A 1978 UK study of advertising codes of ethics from around the world came to similar conclusions. It found that :

- industry will dedicate resources to code administration only if it expects benefits such as consumer goodwill or the removal of government regulation;

- industry will pay lip service to codes but may not change its behaviour where profits are at issue;

- code enforcement mechanisms are more likely to be clandestine and prone to conflict of interest problems than are government regulations.[8]

These critiques suggest that corporate codes of conduct have both strengths and significant weaknesses. If the human rights movement is shifting its focus from governments to private corporate actors, this move should be accompanied by a systematic attempt to resolve the contentious questions surrounding the use of codes and to spell out strategies available to human rights advocates to ensure that adoption of codes is not counterproductive.

The report that follows is the first in a series of two on the role of business in international human rights protection and promotion. This series summarizes the findings of a research study conducted by the Canadian Lawyers Association for International Human Rights (CLAIHR) in late 1996. This first report focusses on the burgeoning literature on codes of conduct in the United States to highlight the strengths and weaknesses of human rights codes of conduct. It then presents the results of a survey conducted by CLAIHR, in association with the International Centre for Human Rights and Democratic Development (ICHRDD), on the prevalence and content of codes of conduct employed by the largest Canadian companies doing business abroad.

Prevalence

Put simply, a business code of conduct is a statement of principles a business agrees to abide by voluntarily over the course of its operations. Corporate codes of conduct have become relatively commonplace in the United States. Surveys in the late 1980s suggest that, at that time, as many as 77% of large US corporations had some sort of corporate code of conduct.[9] This percentage may be as high as 80-85% at present.[10]

The proportion of corporations in Canada that have some sort of corporate code of conduct is also high, though the data are incomplete. A 1981 survey of 125 of the largest Canadian businesses ranked by revenue found that 49% of the 51 responding corporations had "corporate statements of objectives."[11] Another survey of 132 Canadian companies conducted in 1983 found that 56% had written codes of ethics.[12] A more extensive and recent study published in 1992 surveyed 461 firms listed in the 1988 *Financial Post 500*. Of the 225 firms that responded to the survey, 60% reported either having, or being in the process of developing, codes of conduct.[13] Yet, only 75 of the 225 respondents were deemed to have "fairly well-developed codes of ethics" rather than simple credos, corporate mission statements or the like.[14]

Content

For the most part, codes in both Canada and the United States contain measures designed to protect the firm from wrongful acts by its employees. Corporate social responsibility ranks low on the list of code priorities.[15] Further, the justification for the ethical measures included in codes often stems from fear of the legal consequences of getting caught committing illicit acts.[16] In this regard, surveys from the United States suggest that codes seem to focus on illegal acts — acts which have been defined by the law as punishable (for example, overcharging, bribing, and manipulating accounting books and records). Most of the codes fail to address immoral acts or issues such as executive character, product quality, or civic responsibility. Very few of the codes indicate what behaviour is acceptable under specific circumstances.[17]

At least part of the impetus in the United States for developing corporate codes comes from the recommendations of the 1987 Treadway Commission that companies develop ethics codes to avoid fraud, and an initiative by US defence contractors to clean up their reputation for poor business practices.[18] Also important is the fact that corporations in the US can obtain reductions in fines for such offenses as fraud if they have an ethics program.[19]

The 1992 Canadian survey revealed that the majority of Canadian codes deal with the following areas: relations with the Canadian government; relations with customers/suppliers; payments to government officials; bribes and kickbacks; conflict of interest; firm trade secrets; insider trader information; personal integrity and ethics; and integrity of the financial books. A large minority of codes deal with occupational health and safety. A smaller minority of codes deal with relations with competitors, relations with foreign governments, relations with investors and consumers, environmental affairs, civic and community affairs, and product safety and quality. Many codes also mentioned employee legal responsibility.

This breakdown suggests that Canadian codes resemble their US counterparts in concentrating mainly on issues of immediate concern to the firm and areas where non-compliance by the firm might cause it to run afoul of laws and regulations. The 1992 survey concluded as follows: "...the focus of Canadian corporate codes of ethics is protection of the firm. While some of the codes refer to issues of social responsibility, they are mainly concerned with conduct against the firm."[20] This finding is supported by other content analyses of corporate codes that have found that foreign business practices, community and public relations, and environmental protection, as well as areas of interest to employees such as health and safety and non-discrimination, on average, take up only a fifth of the space devoted to the substantive provisions of the code. The remaining four-fifths is generally devoted to conflict of interest, use of corporate assets, and corruption issues.[21]

Effectiveness

Some analyses of the determinants of ethical business behaviour have found that "a code of conduct or corporate policy statement on ethical behaviour...[is] consistently and significantly related to ethical behaviour."[22] The key determinant underlying positive code contributions to ethical behaviour seems to be "management's willingness to enforce such codes."[23] Other observers view code enforceability[24] and company training and communications programs as being essential if codes are to be effective.[25] Mechanisms permitting employees to "whistleblow" on violators without fearing retaliation may also be important.[26]

At the same time, other studies have found that codes of conduct have little effect on actual business behaviour, even in areas of immediate concern to business, such as accounting.[27] For instance, a US study showed that while management in companies with codes are likely to be more concerned with ethics than managers in non-code possessing companies, pressure on employees to manipulate accounts to achieve income targets is greater in companies with written codes than in those without such documents.[28]

In a recent study of 12 Canadian voluntary codes,[29] the Ottawa-based Public Interest Advocacy Centre provided a "mixed verdict" on the effectiveness of voluntary codes.[30] On the positive side, codes were often more responsive to industry differences than was government regulation. Further, consumers often had better access to code administrators than to government regulators and codes allowed diffe-rent stakeholder groups to understand the constraints each faced. At the same time : codes were developed and administered in a fashion giv-ing rise to conflicts of interest between code adherence and business concerns; they were inadequate in their coverage; consumers were generally unaware of their existence; they lacked adequate sanctions for non-compliance; no systemic monitoring of code compliance existed; and studies of adherence to codes found low levels of compliance on the part of businesses. Studies in the United States have echoed this finding, suggesting that "there is a wide gulf between business ethical standards and consumers' needs and preferences."[31]

Anecdotal evidence also supports the conclusion that codes in and of themselves are ineffective. There were at least three significant examples of Canadian corporations reneging on industry codes in 1996. In June, Canadian hard liquor producers in the United States abandoned their half-century promise not to broadcast advertisements for their product.[32] Also that month, Canadian cigarette manufacturers changed their code of conduct to permit advertising closer to schools

after they were cited by anti-tobacco advocates for several violations of the original code banning such practices.[33] Finally, in July, it was revealed that Canada's infant formula producers were no longer adhering to the World Health Organization marketing code on breast milk substitutes.[34]

Concerns regarding the inadequacy of industry voluntary codes have prompted consumer groups to develop a checklist of variables required for a successful code of conduct. Key variables in these lists include:

- Involvement of stakeholders in the development and continuing improvement of the code;

- Transparency of the administration process;

- Administration of the code by an independent agency;

- Strong involvement of all interested parties in the code administration and compliance verification;

- Adequate funding to allow stakeholder participation;

- A role for government in giving credibility to the code by participation in its administration;

- Coverage that includes all business activities and all sectors of an industry;

- Sanctions available not only against employees who breach code provisions but also against the corporate entity and managers;

- Publicity with respect to code development, code administration, complaints procedures, compliance and reports of abuses and reports of sanctions or other remedies;

- Annual reports on the code to be distributed to all interested parties;

- Advance notice of possible sanctions for non-compliance;

- Text of any code and publicity documents drafted in plain language.[35]

The possibility of government regulatory intervention or legal action in cases where voluntary codes fail to remedy perceived problems

is also often viewed as an important variable in encouraging successful industry codes.[36] Thus, several US studies suggest that the effectiveness of the codes depends on the presence of external enforcement mechanisms, such as government regulations.[37] Several other analysts looking at North American codes argue that administration of codes should be conducted by independent bodies able to resolve disputes fairly and level sanctions against code violators.[38]

Empirical surveys of codes have shown that these prerequisites to effectiveness — particularly those relating to monitoring and enforcement — are often absent in company codes of conduct. Most codes rely on employees to enforce them and many lack effective monitoring. Thus, in one US study,[39] 50% of companies with codes relied on employees filing "exception" reports on violations of the code. In 37% of companies, employees were obliged to sign-off on a compliance report once a year. In the remainder of instances, companies employed ombudspersons or counsellors to serve as monitors. Compliance reports were sent to an audit committee 51% of the time, to the CEO 24% of the time and to other management officials in the remainder of instances. While just over half of the companies with codes had measures to verify these compliance reports, fully 84% of these firms relied on internal auditors and/or line management (10%), the firm's legal department (10%) or finance department (10%). Only 31% also called in external auditors to scrutinize compliance. Further, a large minority of codes contain no enforcement provisions. A US Conference Board study conducted in the late 1980s found that 42% of companies with codes outlined no specific penalties for violations of the code.[40]

In the 1992 Canadian study, almost 70% of codes mentioned enforcement or compliance procedures, but "[v]ery few ... codes emphasize or discuss in detail internal oversight and personal integrity."[41] The most common sort of monitoring involved voluntary compliance by employees and/or supervisor surveillance. Companies also relied on legal departments, internal audits and internal watchdog committees. External and independent auditors were used even less frequently than in the United States, with only 13% of firms making any reference to external review in their codes. The vast majority of codes failed to mention penalties for violations.

Codes of Conduct and Human Rights

The literature on corporate codes of conduct discussed above has focussed almost exclusively on domestic codes of conduct and not on codes used by companies to guide their overseas activities. The codes of ethics examined by these studies do not necessarily include reference to human rights, an area of key concern where businesses are operating in jurisdictions with poor human rights environments. The section that follows seeks to remedy this omission by turning its attention to recent developments in human rights codes of conduct. It begins by identifying the human rights that businesses have begun to incorporate in their international codes. It then examines the US experience with these codes of conduct.

International human rights codes of conduct have focussed primarily on labour rights, most of which are defined in international legal instruments. The Organization for Economic Co-operation and Development (OECD), the multilateral economic policy-making body of the industrialized nations, identifies four "core" labour standards found in International Labour Organization (ILO) and United Nations (UN) conventions as human rights.[42] These are:

1. Freedom of Association and the Rights to Organize and Bargain Collectively: employees should be free to join organizations of their liking without prior authorization from the firm and to organize and bargain collectively without fear of retaliation.[43]

2. Non-Discrimination: employees should not be discriminated against on the basis of their race, colour, national origin, sex, religion or other belief, or political or other opinion.[44] Discrimination on the basis of sexual orientation may be an emerging norm that should also be included in this list.[45]

3. Child Labour: employees should not be younger than 14 or than the legally prescribed working age, whichever is higher.[46] The OECD's focus of concern is "exploitative child labour," a phenomena for which a separate international convention has not yet been finalized.[47]

4. Forced Labour: employees should not be forced or compelled to work for the business or to manufacture inputs used by the business.[48]

According to the OECD, violation of these norms is a matter of great humanitarian concern.[49] Moreover, the ILO and UN conventions containing these human rights are widely, though not universally, ratified by states.[50] Subsidiary "labour" standards that many human rights advocates, and US trade law,[51] characterize as key rights are as follows:

1. *Safe and Healthful Work Environment:* employees should be provided with a safe and healthful working environment and not exposed to hazardous conditions.[52]

2. *Fair Wages:* at the very least, employees should be paid minimum wages that meet the basic necessities of life and do not fall below the legal minimum wage, whichever is greater.[53]

3. *Working Hours and Overtime:* employees should not be made to work more than 48 hours a week except under exceptional circumstances and for appropriate overtime compensation.[54]

In addition to referring to this set of rights, or some variant thereof, corporate human rights codes occasionally also include "country guidelines" establishing how the firm will react to situations where human rights violations in a given country are so pervasive that maintaining workplace human rights standards is difficult.

The US Experience

A growing number of well-known US corporations that operate or source globally have begun to introduce codes of conduct referring to many of these human rights standards. In a survey of 150 US multinational corporations in sectors deemed likely to have supplier codes, San Francisco-based Business for Social Responsibility found that 25 firms had human rights codes.[55] Another survey by Boston-based Franklin Research and Development found that roughly 10% of US multinationals had overseas human rights guidelines.[56] A more comprehensive survey on the child labour practices of US retailers and textile manufacturers by the US Department of Labor in 1996 revealed that of 42 major textile retailers and manufacturers surveyed and willing to make public their responses, 36 had adopted some form of policy specifically prohibiting the use of child labour in overseas production facilities.[57] Two of the respondents also had country human rights guidelines that they used to determine which countries they would invest in.[58]

Thirty-seven apparel firms supplied codes of conduct to the US Department of Labor. Content analysis of these codes reveals that many contain other labour rights beyond child labour. The chart below portrays the breakdown by labour right for firms with standards that are more specific than simple "compliance with local laws":

Table 1 US Department of Labor Survey, Results		
Labour Right	**Number of firms**	
Freedom of Association	2	5%
Right to Organize and Bargain Collectively	2	5%
Prohibition of Forced Labour	27	73%
Prohibition of Child Labour	29	78%
Non-discrimination in Employment	19	51%
Safe and Healthful Work Environment	22	59%
Fair Wages	8	22%
Working Hours and Overtime	12	59%

The histories of several of the codes identified in the US Department of Labor study have been well documented and are instructive.

Levi's Code

In 1991, Levi Strauss & Co., the privately-held US clothing manufacturer and retailer, established a management task force — the Sourcing Guidelines Working Group (SGWG) — to draw up Global Sourcing Guidelines that would govern its overseas production. Asked to consider the interests of the company's stakeholders — including its employees, customers and the communities in which it operates — the SGWG devised draft guidelines after reviewing the UN Universal Declaration of Human Rights and other international human rights legal instruments.[59] The company concluded that "[s]ourcing decisions which emphasize cost to the exclusion of all other factors will not best serve our long-term business interests."[60] In the absence of guidelines, the company could "end up with contractors who don't abide by responsible business policies, and our association with them could damage the image of our brands and our company."[61]

In March 1992, following embarrassing revelations in the *Washington Post* of worker abuse at Levi's supplier plants in the Northern Mariana Islands, Levi's introduced sourcing guidelines setting out environmental, ethical, health and safety, and labour standards. These terms apply to contractors and suppliers providing labour or materials to Levi's. According to the Levi Strauss Business Partner Terms of Engagement, Levi's will do business only with partners who: provide wages and benefits complying with local law and matching local practices; do not use child, prison or forced labour or discriminate against groups; or who do not use corporal punishment "or other forms of mental or physical coercion." The Levi's code also contains reference to freedom of association rights.

Levi's has introduced an internal monitoring and enforcement system that includes a detailed questionnaire on supplier employment practices and provides for surprise inspections and the annulment of contracts with violators. Levi's will terminate relationships with suppliers who appear unwilling to improve their practices. Where improvement seems possible, Levi's will set out an improvement plan and timeline and will maintain its relationship with the supplier if the plan's objectives are met. Finally, where all the goals of the guidelines are met, but the supplier could do more, Levi's has committed itself to working to improve performance in order to make the supplier a "model partner." Levi's has cancelled contracts with more than thirty suppliers and required reforms in more than 100 other companies.[62] It has dedicated 50 employees to monitoring workplace conditions at its 450 contractors around the world.[63]

A second facet of Levi's code of conduct is its Guidelines for Country Selection. These touch on human rights, health and safety, and political and social stability issues that stem from the policies of the governments of nations in which Levi's is working. Under the Guidelines, Levi's will assess whether the human rights situation in the country is such that it can expect its contractors to meet its Business Partner Terms of Engagement. Using these principles Levi Strauss & Co. "decided [in 1992] to begin a phased withdrawal from its operations in China, which involve sewing or finishing goods, a process that will continue to completion unless there is a substantial improvement in human rights conditions in the PRC. At the same time, the company decided that it would not initiate direct investment in China."[64]

The Levi's move in China followed cross-checking by auditors of its suppliers against a list of known prison-labour facilities. Levi's also conducted surprise visits[65] and consulted with human rights activists on the situation in China.[66] Similar steps were taken in Burma, the results of which prompted Levi's to pull out of that country as well.[67] When Levi's decides to withdraw from a country using the Guidelines, it undertakes a detailed analysis of the human rights situation in that nation and identifies the improvements that have to be made before the company will return.[68]

Other Codes

Difficulties with the Chinese human rights situation have prompted moves by other companies to employ codes of conduct. For example, in March 1992, Sears, Roebuck and Co. introduced a policy to insure that its imports from China were not made by prison labour. The Sears policy "requires that all contracts that Sears signs for the import of products emanating from China include a clause stating that none of the goods subject to the contract have been manufactured by 'convict or forced labor.'"[69] The policy also indicates that "Sears employees may from time to time conduct unannounced inspections of manufacturing sites in mainland China to determine compliance with US law as regards the use of forced or convict labor." Sears will maintain lists of its suppliers' production facilities to compare with lists of known forced labour camps.

Sears' general code of conduct for its associates also contains wording dealing with suppliers. It indicates that Sears "will only deal with suppliers who share Sears' commitment to the highest ethical business standards and who have proven records of supplying safe, quality products or services that conform with the law. When purchasing goods not produced in the United States, the production facilities, business and labor practices, and merchandise of our suppliers must comply with all applicable local and United States laws."[70]

Reebok, the US shoe producer, has also introduced a code of conduct derived in part from principles developed initially for its operations in China. A long-time supporter of Amnesty International and the sponsor of the "Witness" program that provides human rights advocates with video cameras, computers, and fax machines, Reebok's code states that its devotion "to human rights worldwide is a hallmark of our corporate culture. As a corporation in an ever-more global economy we will not be indifferent to the standards of our business partners around the world."[71] The motivations underlying this approach stem from the company's sensitivity to threats to its reputation.[72] The Reebok code deals with non-discrimination, wages, child labour, occupational health and safety, and, unlike many other codes, freedom of association.

While Reebok continues to operate in China, it prefers joint ventures rather than sourcing from government factories as a means to ensure that its code obligations are met. Reebok argues that "constructive engagement" rather than economic sanctions is the best way to support its worker and human rights standards. "Reebok believes that by maintaining the relationship with a supplier, and the influence that accompanies it, over the long term labor rights and conditions will be improved."[73] According to Reebok, cancelling contracts indirectly punishes workers, a point echoed by the National Labor Committee during its campaign against The Gap when The Gap sought to rescind its contract with its supplier rather than work actively to improve conditions (see below).

Enforcement of the Reebok code is conducted via monitoring by Reebok personnel in the factories, audit teams from Reebok's international headquarters, and oversight by an independent accounting firm that undertakes "payroll audits, interview[s] workers and conduct[s] 'focus groups' on wages and working conditions."[74] Reebok has on at least one occasion "forced a factory in China to relocate workers after discovering safety problems at on-site worker dormitories."[75]

Another shoe producer, Nike, introduced a code of conduct in 1992 — in response to complaints of labour exploitation by foreign suppliers — and in 1994 introduced the "Nike Production Primer" that includes a memorandum of understanding signed by each of its suppliers. The memorandum stipulates that the contractors will respect Nike's codes, not employ forced labour and respect the environment. Similarly, clothing retailer The Gap has had a code of conduct for several years. The code is comprehensive and among the most detailed yet developed. Other US firms with supplier codes of conduct include Home Depot, Timberland, Wal-Mart and JCPenney.[76] The Wal-Mart code was introduced in 1993 after an NBC report showed Bangladeshi child labourers making Wal-Mart shirts.[77]

Criticism of US Corporate Codes

While codes of conduct governing sourcing arrangements represent an acknowledgement by North American firms of their responsibility for the practices of their suppliers, critics contend that most codes have been introduced by corporations, not out of a pre-existing management commitment to social responsibility, but in response to public pressure.[78] Further, critics argue that codes have been of limited effectiveness.

With regard to the first point, since 1984, the United States has introduced a series of unilateral trade measures protecting worker rights overseas that might prove highly disruptive to corporate activities if imposed on nations in which businesses have invested or from which they are sourcing.[79] Other developments include the labour rights regime under the NAFTA side agreement, the prospect of linkages between trade and labour rights in the GATT/WTO,[80] and litigation in US courts stemming from violations of labour rights abroad.[81] Public pressure for corporate social responsibility from consumers has also become more marked, as have demands from shareholders and investors.[82]

With respect to code effectiveness, many observers have argued that corporate human rights codes are mere window-dressing. According to Stephen Coats of the Chicago-based US/Guatemala Labor Education Project, the guidelines are often minimalist, being mostly public relations responses to consumer pressure. Many codes merely require suppliers to obey local laws and pay prevailing wages.[83] Those supplier codes that do include standards on child labour, health and safety, and sustainable wages usually do not also include provisions focussing on the rights of workers to unionize,[84] a finding consistent with the content analysis of apparel industry codes offered above.

In addition, workers are often unaware of the existence of the guidelines. Charles Kernaghan, executive director of the New York-based National Labor Committee Education Fund in Support of Worker and Human Rights in Central America (NLC), reports that workers employed by firms sourced by US retailing giants such as The Gap are oblivious to the existence of these codes.[85] Similarly, the Washington, DC-based *Multinational Monitor* reported in June 1995 that workers in firms associated with Nike's Indonesian operations had never seen the Nike code.[86] These findings are consistent with those made by the US

Department of Labor in its 1996 study of 42 major US textile firms: "only a very few respondents indicated that they have tried to ensure that production workers in overseas facilities know about their code or policy by specifically requiring that copies of such a statement be posted. Only three companies stated that they unconditionally require contractors to post their code."[87] Indeed, "meetings [between workers in overseas factories and US Department of Labor officials]...suggested that relatively few workers are aware of the existence of codes of conduct, and even fewer understand their implications."[88]

Most critically, while large retail corporations such as The Gap, JCPenney, Levi's, Nike and others are often major purchasers — and in some cases the sole purchaser — able to exert significant influence on their suppliers, retail companies have proven ineffectual in policing their own codes, frequently overlooking important transgressions, including violations of local labour laws. In this regard, JCPenney sourcing factories in Guatemala have apparently employed child labourers, a practice the company failed to check on despite its code of conduct.[89] Levi Strauss allegedly used child labour, failed to pay wages and allowed unsafe working conditions in its Juarez, Mexico supplier plant[90] and was accused of not meeting its own standards on labour organizing at supplier factories in Honduras.[91] The company has gone on record as saying that its inspectors often miss infractions of its code "because, to avoid offending factory owners, they don't delve too deeply."[92] Reebok was criticized for its operations in Indonesia, where its prevailing wages were deemed to be below subsistence levels.[93] Workers in Nike's Indonesian supplier factories have sometimes been physically and mentally abused by management and denied wages, investigatory reports suggest.[94] Finally, so severe were the discrepancies between the codes of conduct touted by retailers operating in Central America and the on-the-ground reality in the source plants that, at one point, US human rights groups contemplated bringing suit in the US against at least one retailer for consumer fraud.[95]

Experience in Guatemala has suggested that retail companies are most effective in ensuring supplier adherence to codes where independent observers monitor compliance. In one instance identified by Stephen Coats, workers fired from the *Confecciones Unidas Maquiladora* in Guatemala City were reinstated at the behest of Sears, Wal-Mart and JCPenney after being notified about the incident by the US/Guatemala Labor Education Project. Working conditions at the

Cigne-owned JMB apparel *maquiladora* also improved following an investigation by the US-based Working Assets social investment firm.[96] The conclusions of human rights groups in Latin America regarding code effectiveness is echoed by Canadian union activists pressing for more robust labour standards in Asia: codes of conduct are meaningless public relations exercises without independent monitoring and enforcement mechanisms.[97]

The US Department of Labor study of 42 US textile firms suggests that effective monitoring of codes remains uncommon. The study concluded that "most of the codes of the respondents do not contain detailed provisions for monitoring and implementation, and many of these companies do not have a reliable monitoring system in place."[98] Overseas investigation by the Department revealed that "[w]hile monitoring for product quality, and even for health and safety conditions, is customary in the garment industry, the field visits by Department of Labor officials suggest that monitoring for compliance with provisions of the codes of conduct of US garment importers dealing with other labor standards — and child labor in particular — is not."[99] Where there is monitoring "there seems to be relatively little interaction between, on the one hand, monitors, and on the other hand, workers and the local community. It also appears that monitors have a technical background in production and quality control and are relatively untrained with regard to implementation of labor standards."[100]

Independent Monitoring: The Next Frontier

In December 1995, the National Labor Committee Education Fund in Support of Worker and Human Rights in Central America (NLC) scored an important victory in its efforts to curb exploitative labour practices by sweatshop textile manufacturers in Central America. The Gap clothing stores, brought to the table by the NLC's heated consumer protest campaign, finally agreed to place conditions on its purchases of clothing from a key supplier, El Salvador-based Mandarin International.

Mandarin, a Taiwanese firm supplying JCPenney, Eddie Bauer, Dayton-Hudson, Wal-Mart and Gitano as well as The Gap, had been accused of abusing its 900 workers, using child labour and paying "starvation wages." In June 1995, the company fired 186 workers from its El Salvador plant in the San Marcos Free Trade Zone for their involvement in the area's first union. At about the same time, union leaders were kidnapped and tortured by unknown assailants.[101]

The National Labor Committee's 1995 campaign focussing on the activities of The Gap supplier Mandarin International included a North American speaking tour by two former Mandarin workers that spawned over a 100 public demonstrations and pickets of The Gap stores and letter-writing campaigns by consumers and members of the religious community.[102]

Called a "watershed" by then US Labor Secretary Robert Reich,[103] the statement of resolution eventually signed by The Gap and the NLC in New York on December 15, 1995, required that Mandarin meet with union members to resolve their differences in the office of the Salvadoran Labour Ministry. On the table was the reinstatement of the fired workers.

In an unprecedented move, The Gap also agreed that independent human rights monitors in El Salvador would be free to monitor source plant compliance with the company's Sourcing Principles and Guidelines. In the long term, a separate independent codes monitoring body may be established via negotiations to be conducted by The Gap, the New-York-based Interfaith Center for Corporate Responsibility (ICCR), and San Francisco-based Business for Social Responsibility (BSR). No other company has permitted external evaluation of its adherence to codes of conduct, says Charles Kernaghan, executive director of the NLC, and the measure was strongly opposed by the retailer lobby, the US National Retailers Association. In another important move, The Gap agreed to translate its code of conduct into Spanish and post it in its source plants, despite the objections of other industry members.

The agreement is not a legal contract. However, Kernaghan expects The Gap to act in good faith rather than risk a renewal of the NLC's damaging campaign against the company.[104] While Mandarin International is not bound by the agreement, it is understood that should a fair settlement with workers not be arrived at, The Gap will no longer do business with the company. The threat of losing US firms as a customer is probably a significant impetus for suppliers to meet standards. In the words of the US Department of Labor, "[c]ontinued access to the US market is a very large incentive for overseas garment producers to meet quality/timeliness requirements and comply with codes of conduct."[105]

The Gap's concessions to the NLC and its Salvadoran partners open the door to institutionalizing independent confirmation of labour standards in all of The Gap's source plants. Following the December 15 Resolution, the Independent Monitoring Working Group (IMWG) was formed, made up of representatives of BSR, the NLC, The Gap and the ICCR. Since that time, the IMWG — through consultations with US and international human rights, labour, religious, academic and business groups — has arrived at the following working definition of independent monitoring:

> An effective process of direct observation and information-gathering by credible and respected institutions and individuals to ensure compliance with corporate codes of conduct and applicable laws to prevent violations, process grievances, and promote humane, harmonious, and productive workplace conditions.[106]

The IMWG has also established the following goals for the monitoring to be performed at the Mandarin facility:

- detect violations of The Gap's Sourcing Principles and Guidelines and applicable local law;

- promote practices leading to compliance with The Gap's Sourcing Principles and Guidelines and applicable local law;

- encourage Mandarin to educate managers and workers about The Gap's Sourcing Principles and Guidelines, applicable laws, their own responsibilities, and the rights of workers;

- deter abuses against workers;

- provide a safe, fair, credible, and efficient mechanism for dispute resolution;

- promote utilization of existing processes within the factory to resolve problems where possible.[107]

In March 1996, another resolution was signed by Mandarin and representatives of several Salvadoran groups involved in the monitoring arrangement setting out the composition of the Mandarin monitoring body — the International Monitoring Group of El Salvador (GMIES) — and agreeing on a schedule for the reinstatement of the fired workers.

As of August 1996, GMIES had monitors living at the Mandarin site and conducting interviews with Mandarin workers. It had declared the company in compliance with The Gap's code. In September 1996, however, in light of further difficulties, a new document was signed to establish a productive situation in the factory and to ensure the reinstatement of appropriate personnel in a harmonious manner. Some ex-union leaders have been reinstated since then, as well as a number of workers. The IMWG is considering extending the independent monitoring system to Honduras and Guatemala.[108] In the meantime, The Gap has begun placing new orders with the factory. The IMWG views The Gap's continued patronage of Mandarin as essential if the monitoring initiative is to succeed.[109]

In conclusion, human rights codes of conduct are becoming increasingly popular among US firms, particularly those selling consumer products. At the same time, these codes suffer from several shortcomings, particularly in the area of monitoring and enforcement. These findings replicate those identified with respect to domestic codes of conduct.

While studies on the overseas human rights codes of conduct of US firms are becoming more common, information on the international human rights practices of Canadian firms has been virtually non-existent. The 1992 Canadian survey cited above revealed that 28 of the 75 codes of conduct submitted by the respondents were not Canada or US-specific in their content. For its part, the 1983 study indicated that 60% of the 51 firms responding to the questionnaire would apply similar social responsibility standards in both Canada and abroad. It was unclear from these responses whether corporations applied universal standards or merely abided by the potentially differing laws of each jurisdiction. Neither survey dealt with international human rights issues. As a consequence, no published study has yet examined Canadian corporate codes of conduct with respect to human rights issues in the overseas operations of Canadian firms.

CLAIHR/ICHRDD Survey

Between June and October 1996, at the request of ICHRDD, CLAIHR surveyed 110 Canadian firms to ascertain whether these corporations had codes of conduct applicable to their international activities and including reference to core labour rights. The survey sought to elicit information on

- how many of Canada's largest businesses by sector had codes of conduct extending to their international activities;

- what issues these codes focussed on;

- whether Canadian international codes contained reference to the four core labour rights identified by the OECD;[110]

- how codes were monitored and enforced;

- whether businesses believed that they had a role to play in promoting international human rights protection and sustainable development.

Methodology

The 110 corporations selected for the survey were drawn from the sector rankings provided by the *Globe and Mail's Report on Business,* July 1995 and the *Financial Post 500,* Summer 1995. Selected corporations ranked among the top firms in the following non-financial sectors: Integrated Oils; Chemicals; Integrated Mines; Metal and other Mines; Gold Producers; Forest Products; Food Retailers; Consumer Products; Retailers; Utilities; Wholesalers; General Manufacturers; Automotive; Conglomerates; and Hi-Tech. Of all the sectors found in the *Report on Business* and *Financial Post,* these industries were viewed as those most likely to have overseas operations or sourcing arrangements with a significant labour component. It was felt that while financial services companies, for example, do go abroad, their operations are not labour intensive, nor are they as likely to be attracted to invest internationally by differential labour or environmental conditions, which is the focus of this study. While the impact on human rights of financial lending practices is a legitimate concern, this was viewed as being more properly the focus of another study.

Each of the corporations listed in the sector rankings for these sectors in the *Report on Business* and *Financial Post* was researched to determine whether they were involved in one or more of the following pursuits:

- foreign direct investment — whether in terms of resource extraction, exploration, or manufacturing — in countries in Latin America, Africa, Eastern Europe or Asia;

- joint ventures — whether in terms of resource extraction, exploration, or manufacturing — in countries in Latin America, Africa, Eastern Europe or Asia;

- sourcing or purchasing relationships with suppliers in Latin America, Africa, Eastern Europe or Asia.

The following sources were used to determine whether the business in question was engaged in any of these activities:

- *Blue Book of Canadian Business* (Canadian Newspaper Service, 1995);

- *Canada Company Handbook* (*Report on Business*, 1995);

- Compac-Disclosure CD-ROM (Annual Reports and disclosure documents of 8,000 Canadian corporations);

- *Financial Post Survey of Industrials* (Financial Post, 1995);

- *Financial Post Survey of Mines and Energy Resources* (Financial Post, 1995).

Where there was no indication from these source materials that the company was participating in any of the three pursuits listed above, that company was excluded from the study. Exceptions were made for retailers and wholesalers. Firms from these sectors were included even if the sources did not report sourcing arrangements with suppliers in the developing world. It was reasoned that contractual import relationships were unlikely to be reported in the sources listed above. Since the involvement of retailers and wholesalers with developing countries is often through such supplier relationships, reliance on the sources would result in these sectors being improperly excluded from the study. Further, as the discussion above indicates, these are the sectors whose overseas supplier labour codes have received the most attention over the last several years.

Final differences in the number of firms surveyed in each of the sectors stemmed largely from differences in the initial numbers of firms listed in the sector breakdowns provided in the *Financial Post* and the *Report on Business*. Yet, the firm selection process also revealed that sectors vary with respect to the likelihood that firms will operate internationally. For example, a large proportion of the mining companies identified in the *Financial Post* and *Report on Business* lists operate internationally and thus were included in the survey. Conversely, only a small number of the manufacturing firms identified in the lists appear to have operations outside of Canada.

Each company was phoned to determine who at the firm would be able to do the survey. The questionnaire and a stamped return envelope were then mailed to this person. The cover letter accompanying the questionnaire introduced CLAIHR and ICHRDD and explained the purpose of the survey. Recipients were informed that their responses would be made public in this report.

Once the due date for the return of questionnaires had passed, each company that had not returned the form was phoned to remind them of the due date. Companies were phoned a total of four times between mid-August and mid-September before they were deemed non-respondents. In many instances, companies who indicated that they had not received the mailed questionnaire were faxed another copy. A third copy was faxed to many firms who reported not having received the questionnaire after the first round of faxes. Companies who declined to return the questionnaire were interviewed over the phone to determine the reasons for their unwillingness to participate.

Response Rate

Of the 110 firms surveyed, 12 indicated that they did not, in fact, operate in any of the geographic areas identified in the questionnaire or had ceased operations in these regions. As a consequence, 98 firms were deemed part of the proper survey sample. Twenty-one businesses provided a detailed description of their codes of conduct in their returned questionnaire. Only seven of these firms actually supplied a copy of their code. An eighth code was obtained from other sources after the survey. Another six companies did not complete their question-naire, but sent their codes of conduct. A further four companies said during the phone interview that they were reviewing or introducing codes of conduct. Twelve other companies indicated during the follow-up call that they did not have codes. Some of these companies reported that they did, as a matter of policy, apply some standards of relevance to this study. Another 19 firms did not fill out the questionnaire and were unwilling, or unable, to provide more information over the phone for an assortment of reasons. The final 36 firms did not return the questionnaire and either did not respond to our repeated telephone inquiries or promised to send the questionnaire on several occasions but never did. The survey response rates can be summarized as follows:

Table 2 Summary of Response Statistics	
Number of companies initially selected for the study	110
Number of companies initially selected not operating in the relevant regions	12
Number of companies retained	98
Number of companies providing no response to the survey	55
Number of companies responding to the survey	43
Number of companies completing the questionnaire	21
Number of companies who did not complete the questionnaire, but who sent in codes	6
Number of companies contacted by phone who have, or are preparing, codes	4
Number of companies contacted by phone who do not have codes	12

With regard to response rate by sector, mineral resource and energy companies had the highest response rate. Seventeen of 32 mining companies in the 98-firm survey sample were respondents. Nine of these completed the questionnaire. Seven of the firms returning questionnaires had codes. The response rate of oil and chemical companies was also relatively high. Five of eight oil and gas and chemical firms in the survey sample were deemed respondents. Four of these firms completed the questionnaire. Two of three utilities surveyed responded to the survey and returned questionnaires. Response rates from other sectors were less pronounced. Four of 11 manufacturing and automotive businesses responded to the survey. Only one of these firms completed the questionnaire. Out of nine hi-tech firms surveyed, five responded and three filled out the questionnaire. The response rate among "Consumer Producers," a composite of wholesalers, retailers, food stores, and household and consumer product producers, was fairly low. Eight of 29 firms responded to the survey, with four firms returning questionnaires. Neither of the two forestry companies in the survey provided a response. One of the two service firms contacted responded, but did not return the questionnaire. One of the two conglomerates surveyed did respond but did not return a questionnaire. Response rates by sector are portrayed in chart form below:

Table 3 Response Rates by Sector

Sector	Number of companies in survey sample	Number of responses	Number of returned questionnaires from firms with codes
Mining	32	17	7
Oil and Chemical	8	5	4
Manufacturing and Automotive	11	4	1
Utilities	3	2	2
Hi-Tech	9	5	3
Consumer Producers	29	8	4
Forestry	2	0	0
Services and Conglomerates	4	2	0
Totals	98	43	21

Results

Prevalence of Codes of Conduct.

Of the 98 firms in the survey, 55 declined to both complete the questionnaire and indicate over the telephone whether they had codes of conduct. Forty-three firms did respond to the questionnaire or to the phone survey. This gave the survey a 44% response rate. A total of 34 of these 43 firms had — or were introducing — codes of conduct (79%), a figure consistent with the studies discussed in Chapter 1 above. Twenty-one of these companies explicitly indicated that they had codes that applied to their overseas operations. In other words, 49% of the 43 respondent companies reported having international codes of conduct.

It is unclear how this figure should be interpreted. As other analysts have observed in previous surveys, firms with codes are probably more prone to complete surveys than are non-code firms.[111] Firms without codes may not wish to make this fact known in a public report and might prefer to be recorded as non-respondents. If we assume that most of the firms that did not respond to the survey do not have codes, then the percentage of the largest Canadian international businesses by sector with some sort of international codes of conduct may be as low as 21%.

Detailed breakdown of the survey results are found in Tables 4 through 8. Table 5, on page 48, provides a sector by sector breakdown for the codes of companies that responded to the questionnaire. Table 6 presents the same data, but by company. Table 7 contrasts the questionnaire responses and the actual code contents for the seven firms who both completed a questionnaire and supplied their code of conduct, along with the one obtained after the survey Table 8 provides the results of the telephone survey of firms who did not return the questionnaire or who provided a questionnaire but indicated that they did not have a code.

Minimal Standards

As Table 6 shows, of the 21 firms that returned questionnaires, 17 contemplate applying Canadian, corporate, or international standards to their operations in regions where labour and environmental standards are lower than those in Canada. Another five firms who do not have codes indicate that they apply Canadian or North American standards. Thus, of the 43 respondents, 51% (22) report that they will apply more stringent standards where local standards are less strict than the norms the company applies in the Canadian context. This finding suggests that at least 21% of all the 98 firms surveyed apply some sort of minimal labour and environmental standards reflective of those employed in Canada.

Code Provisions

Results from the content questions of the 21 returned questionnaires are portrayed in Table 5, broken down by sector.[112] Generally speaking, the codes of the 21 firms that returned the questionnaire focus on business practice issues such as bribery and supplier relations. Many also focus on environmental protection, worker health and safety, and relations with customers. A number of codes include reference to relations with employees.

With the exception of non-discrimination, the majority of codes do not include reference to the OECD core labour human rights. Indeed, the firm-specific breakdown in Table 6 indicates that only six of 21 corporations include direct or implied reference to all of these rights in their codes. Thus, 14% of the 43 responding firms have codes of conduct referring to all the OECD's core labour rights. This figure falls to 6% for the survey as a whole if one assumes that the 55 non-responding firms do not have such codes. Of the 43 companies returning the questionnaire, 14% (6) report having some sort of policy relating to operations in countries with oppressive regimes. This figure translates into 6% of the 98 surveyed firms.

Only two of the six companies that indicated on the questionnaire that they had codes referring to all core labour standards actually provided a code. As Table 7 shows, the codes of these companies — Inco and Hydro-Québec — contain few, if any, reference to core labour standards. In fairness, the code sent by Inco is expressly an environmental statement of principles. It may be that Inco has another code that it failed to send. Hydro-Québec, meanwhile, simply indicated in the questionnaire that it applies all core labour standards set out in international treaties adhered to by Canada in all its operations. It had not distilled this commitment into writing in its code.

The Ontario Hydro International code, obtained after the survey, is much more impressive. With the exception of the right to organize and bargain collectively, the code does contain very explicit reference to the core labour standards as well as fair wages, working conditions, and health and safety. It is unclear whether the "freedom of association in the workplace" invoked in the code encompasses the right to organize and bargain collectively. The response on the questionnaire, where the latter right was circled, suggests that it probably does. It also mentions the rights of women and of indigenous and tribal people and indicates that Ontario Hydro International "will not be complicit in projects in which there are gross human rights violations." The code applies directly to all Ontario Hydro employees and business partners. Further, Ontario Hydro International "will not knowingly purchase materials or contract services that involve breaches of any of the above human rights or social justice provisions."

Code Monitoring

As Table 6 indicates, the most frequent monitoring devices associated with codes are internal audits, employed by 16 of the 21 firms who completed the questionnaire, and reliance on corporate legal counsel (16 companies). Supervisor surveillance is also common (12 companies), while internal oversight committees are used in a minority of cases (seven companies). Independent audits are the least frequently used monitoring systems (six companies). Finally, 12 of the 21 firms offer some sort of whistleblower protection or have an anonymous reporting system. Table 7, contrasting the content of the codes that were supplied by questionnaire respondents with the questionnaires themselves, suggests that many of these monitoring devices are not expressly identified in the codes themselves. Table 7 also shows that while Ontario Hydro reported reliance on internal audits in its questionnaire, its code refers to independent audits: "periodic, project or process-specific independent audits, including ongoing assessments of the impact of major projects on local communities, will be conducted to ensure compliance with the ... Code of Ethics."

Ethics Reporting and Employee Training

Only five of the 21 firms (24%) issue ethics reports to shareholders or other stakeholders. Eleven of the 21 firms (52%) offer some sort of employee training related to the code of conduct.

Business Role in Human Rights Promotion and Sustainable Development

Firms were asked whether they believed business had a role to play in protecting international human rights and promoting sustainable development. None of the 21 firms disagreed with this statement. Sixteen agreed that business has such a role. Two firms that do not have codes also agreed with this statement. Thus, of the 43 respondents to written and telephone surveys, at least 42% felt that human rights protection and sustainable development concern business.

Many firms included more details with their responses to this question. At least one company (Hydro-Québec) felt that the role of business in human rights protection should be self-regulated in a fashion that does not amount to a barrier to trade. Several other firms, including Alcan, Aur Resources, Mark's Work Wearhouse, Ontario Hydro and Placer Dome, felt that business should play a guiding and facilitative role. Inco indicated that "Canadian companies operating abroad should work to the highest standard of ethics and environmental excellence." Hudson's Bay agreed that business should adhere to international standards and participate in developing guidelines but that government should remain the key player.

Table 4 Summary of Key Results	
Number of companies reporting codes of conduct	34 (79%)
Number of companies reporting international codes of conduct	21 (49%)
Number of companies applying more rigourous environmental and labour standards where host country standards are lower than those in Canada	22 (51%)
Number of companies with codes containing *all* OECD core labour rights	6 (14%)
Number of companies with codes containing *some* OECD core labour rights	13 (32%)
Number of companies with codes dealing with operations in countries with oppressive regimes	6 (14%)
Number of companies who use independent audits to oversee and enforce codes	6 (14%)
Number of companies who offer "whistleblower" protection to persons who report code violations	12 (30%)
Number of companies who believe business has a role to play in protecting international human rights and promoting sustainable development	18 (42%)

Discussion

A number of important conclusions can be drawn from this survey. First, the vast majority of Canada's largest international businesses either do not have or, at the time of this survey, were not willing to talk about international codes of conduct. Only 21 of 98 companies surveyed expressly reported having codes or ethical guidelines that applied to their international operations.

At its most banal, this finding suggests that Canadian business places a very low priority on communicating its response to issues it confronts in its overseas operations to the non-governmental sector. Some firms simply were unable to find the time to complete the survey, though they expressed interest in the human rights subject matter of the survey. On the other hand, a large number of firms expressed no such interest. If one assumes — as other researchers have — that a failure to respond to repeated phone inquiries reflects a disinterest, not only in the survey, but in its subject matter as well, these results imply that business interest in devising an international human rights policy is low.

Second, the actual results of the survey suggest that businesses have not placed social responsibility and human rights codes high on their priority list. A minority of the respondent firms had codes that contained guidelines on community relations (12 firms, 28% of respondent companies), and environmental protection (17 firms, 40% of respondent companies). Just over half (22 firms, 51%) of respondent firms indicated that they will apply more stringent environmental and labour standards where local standards are less rigorous than Canadian norms. Further, of the 21 firms that reported having international codes of conduct, only 11 offered employee training on the codes, a finding that suggests that many of the shortcomings in code promotion and awareness identified in the US context may also apply to Canadian firms. It is also notable that external or independent audits — a monitoring device viewed as essential by many critics of codes — are used by only six of the 21 firms returning the questionnaire.

Most critically for this study, the results indicate that only six (14%) of the 43 respondent firms (6% of the 98 firms surveyed) have some sort of policy concerning dealings with oppressive regimes. A similar, small proportion of companies have codes of conduct that refer to all the OECD core labour rights. These four labour rights are the most basic standards, violations of which are — according to the OECD — a matter of great humanitarian concern. It is also notable that none of the companies that indicated it had a code containing all of these standards provided a document that actually contained reference to these rights. This oversight makes it impossible to gauge the adequacy of the code provisions or compare them with the international standards or the US codes discussed above. We must also assume that companies did not misrepresent the content of their codes. It is interesting to note, in this regard, that there are discrepancies between questionnaire responses and the handful of codes actually provided by questionnaire respondents, a point demonstrated by the analysis in Table 7. It should be noted, however, that the one code that was obtained after the survey — that of Ontario Hydro International — compares favourably with the US codes in terms of its content and its reliance on independent monitoring.

The insufficiencies of some of the responses aside, the survey does have certain other limitations. First, it is difficult to compare the findings of this survey with the US figures described above. The US surveys differed in their methodology and in their focus. The most comprehensive survey is that conducted by the US Department of Labor in 1996. Unfortunately, this study focused on child labour standards among the largest firms in the apparel industry, a sector which had a very poor response rate in the CLAIHR/ICHRDD survey. Only the following weak comparison can be made between the two surveys: Three out of eight (38%) "consumer producers" responding to the CLAIHR/ICHRDD survey had codes dealing with child labour. The comparable figure for US apparel industry survey was 36 out of 43 (84%). Consumer producers are an agglomeration of sectors that might be expected to have business practices analogous to those in the apparel industry. A comparison of the findings for all Canadian sectors with the single sector of US data is more problematic and thus of little value.

Second, the survey does not assess the on-the-ground application of codes or corporate minimal standards. At the same time, a comparison of the survey's findings as to content with other studies that assess the prerequisites of effective codes suggests that the codes studied in the context of this survey may be flawed. Particularly notable is the absence of rigorous workplace promotion and independent monitoring of the codes. On a more anecdotal level, recent controversy over the environmental practices of two survey respondents suggest that there is reason to suspect that there are discrepancies between corporate principles expressed in the survey and actual behaviour. In this regard, Montreal-based Cambior, a company that reports having environmental standards in its code of conduct, was implicated in a massive tailings spill in Guyana in 1995 that sent an estimated three billion litres of cyanide tainted waters into the country's largest river.[113] Meanwhile in 1996, Placer Dome's subsidiary Marcopper was associated with a disastrous tailings spill in the Philippines, despite the mother company's strong showing on the survey questionnaire.[114]

CONCLUSION

In concluding their study of child labour and codes of conduct in the US apparel industry, the US Department of Labor described corporate codes of conduct as

> a new and promising approach that can contribute to the elimination of child labor in the global garment industry. They involve the private sector — rather than governments and international organizations — in developing solutions to this complex problem.[115]

At the same time, the study cautioned that "[i]t is important to keep in mind ... that codes of conduct are not a panacea."[116] The warning is particularly significant in light of the limitations on actual implementation and enforcement of codes identified by the study and other observers.

This report has examined human rights codes of conduct employed by US firms in their overseas operations. It also represents a first effort to measure the prevalence and content of human rights codes of conduct in the Canadian context. The report suggests that the largest Canadian companies, like many of their US counterparts, are beginning to consider human rights issues in their international practices. This awareness is gratifying. At the same time, the report flags a number of shortcomings in codes of conduct that may reduce their utility. First, the study suggests that the majority of large Canadian businesses operating or sourcing abroad do not have codes containing reference to even the most basic human rights standards. Second, most codes lack the independent monitoring requirements viewed as essential by many code analysts. Third, companies appear to be reluctant to share their codes with the public, even when they report having codes containing human rights language. This recalcitrance runs counter to the call for transparency in code development, implementation and administration promoted by code analysts.

This report also raises the question of what inducements drive businesses to adopt codes and how business implementation and observance of codes can be promoted. The second publication in this series will take up this question by looking at how companies can be encouraged to remedy code shortcomings identified here to better ensure that Canadian companies operating abroad respect basic human rights.

QUESTIONNAIRE ADDRESSED TO CANADIAN COMPANIES

Thank you for participating in the CLAIHR/ICHRDD corporate codes of conduct survey. This survey has been designed to take very little of your time and consists largely of multiple choice questions. We would be grateful to you if you would complete the following questionnaire by circling the appropriate response and providing comments where appropriate and returning the questionnaire to us in the stamped, self-addressed envelope by August 12, 1996. If possible, we would be grateful to you if you would include your codes of conduct and/or ethical guidelines when returning the survey to us. Questions can be addressed to Craig Forcese, CLAIHR, at (613) 233-0398.

Business Name:

1. Does your business operate in, or source raw materials or products from, any of the following regions?

    1. South Asia   5. Africa
    2. East Asia   6. Eastern Europe
    3. South East Asia   7. South or Central America
    4. Caribbean

    Comments:

2. Does your business have ethical guidelines or codes of conduct?

    Yes ☐   No ☐

    Comments:

3. If no, is your firm presently developing ethical guidelines or codes of conduct?

    Yes ☐   No ☐

    If yes, when are your business' guidelines due to be implemented? :

4. Is your business' code of conduct drawn from model industry or sector codes of conduct (ie. CERES Principles, International Chamber of Commerce Business Charter for Sustainable Development, etc.)?

Yes ☐   No ☐

If yes, which code(s) serve(s) as a model?

5. Do the guidelines or codes of conduct apply to your operations or sourcing practices in any of the regions identified in question 1?

Yes ☐   No ☐   n/a ☐

Comments:

6. Where environmental and labour standards are lower in the regions identified in question 1 than in Canada, does your business apply environmental and labour standards developed for Canada while operating in the regions in question 1 or host national standards?

Canadian standards ☐   Host national standards ☐

Comments:

7. Which of the following areas are dealt with in your business' guidelines or codes of conduct? (Please circle relevant areas.) (If you prefer, we will use the codes of conduct you mail to us with the returned questionnaire to answer this question.)

Government Relations
1. Relations with Canadian governments
2. Relations with foreign governments
3. Lobbying and political contributions
4. Bribery and kickbacks
5. Operations in countries with oppressive regimes

Stakeholder Relations
6. Relations with customers
7. Relations with suppliers
8. Relations with employees in Canada
9. Relations with employees abroad
10. Worker health and safety
11. Worker unionization

12. Relations with investors

13. Relations with communities

14. Environmental protection

15. Product safety

16. Product quality

Other (please specify):

8. **Does your business' ethical guidelines or codes of conduct refer to any of the following "core labour standards" identified by the Organization for Economic Co-operation and Development (Please circle relevant areas.)**

   a. Freedom of association

   b. Right to organize and bargain collectively

   c. Prohibition on forced labour

   d. Elimination of child labour exploitation

   e. Non-discrimination in employment

   Comments:

9. **How does your business oversee and enforce its ethical guidelines or codes of conduct? (Please circle relevant areas.)**
   1. Internal audits

   2. Independent audits

   3. Supervisor surveillance

   4. Internal committee

   5. Corporate legal counsel

   Other (please specify):

10. **Does your business issue ethics reports to shareholders or other key stakeholders?**

   Yes ☐   No ☐

   If yes, please include details:

11. **Does your business offer training to employees on the ethical guidelines or codes of conduct?**

   Yes ☐   No ☐

   If yes, please include details:

12. Does your business offer guarantees of non-retaliation to "whistleblowing" employees (persons who report violations of the guidelines or codes of conduct)?

Yes ☐   No ☐

Comments:

13. Does your business believe that international business has a role to play in promoting international human rights protection and sustainable development?

Yes ☐   No ☐

If so, what role should business play?

Table 5 Content of Code, by Sector
(Data from questionnaire and/or code where supplied with questionnaire)

Code Provisions		Mining (7 firms)	C. P.* (4 firms)	Utilities (2 firms)	Hi-Tech (3 firms)	Oil & Gas (4 firms)	M ** (1 firm)	ALL SECTORS (21 firms)
			* Consumer Producers				** Manufacturing	
Relations with Govs.	Relations with Canadian govs.	5/7	1/4	1/2	2/3	2/4	0/1	11/21
	Relations with foreign govs.	6/7	1/4	1/2	2/3	2/4	1/1	13/21
	Lobbying and political contribution	6/7	2/4	1/2	2/3	3/4	1/1	15/21
	Bribery and kickbacks	6/7	4/4	2/2	2/3	3/4	1/1	18/21
	Operations in countries with oppressive regimes	3/7	1/4	1/2	0/3	1/4	0/1	6/21
Relations with Stake-holders	Relations with consumers	3/7	4/4	1/2	3/3	3/4	1/1	15/21
	Relations with suppliers	6/7	4/4	1/2	3/3	3/4	1/1	18/21
	Relations with employees in Canada	5/7	2/4	2/2	2/3	3/4	1/1	15/21
	Relations with employees abroad	5/7	2/4	1/2	2/3	3/4	1/1	14/21
	Worker health and safety	6/7	3/4	2/2	2/3	4/4	1/1	18/21
	Worker unionization	3/7	2/4	0/2	1/3	1/4	0/1	7/21
	Relations with investors	3/7	3/4	1/2	2/3	2/4	1/1	12/21
	Relations with community	5/7	3/4	1/2	1/3	2/4	0/1	12/21
	Environmental protection	6/7	3/4	1/2	2/3	4/4	1/1	17/21
	Product safety	2/7	3/4	1/2	1/3	2/4	1/1	10/21
	Product quality	2/7	3/4	1/2	1/3	1/4	1/1	9/21
Core Labour Rights	Freedom of association	3/7	3/4	2/2	0/3	0/4	0/1	8/21
	Right to organize & bargain collectively	3/7	2/4	2/2	1/3	1/4	0/1	9/21
	Prohibition on forced labour	3/7	1/4	2/2	0/3	0/4	0/1	6/21
	Elimination of child labour exploitation	3/7	3/4	2/2	0/3	0/4	0/1	8/21
	Non-discrimination in employment	4/7	2/4	2/2	2/3	2/4	1/1	13/21

Notes for Tables 6 & 7

1   Company applies the state of the art standards (often US).

2   Core labour rights not officially referenced in code but, in practice company strives to maintain Western standards in its overseas work.

3   Company has an audit committee of the Board of Directors that also deals with the code.

4   Company applies own standards which are sometimes higher than Canadian standards.

5   Company performs annual reviews.

6   Company is developing model codes with Retail Council of Canada and the ILO.

7   Company applies host national standards unless they are viewed as unconscionable, in which case higher standards are applied.

8   Company's ethical standards are applied to sourcing partners.

9   Company applies all core labour standards "with some sensitivity." Child labour exploitation is absolutely prohibited.

10   Code models drawn from the International Chamber of Commerce (ICC) Charter and through consultation with the University of Ottawa Human Rights Centre.

11   Company uses a "proportionality analysis" to determine which standards are appropriate.

12   Responsability of employees to bring notice of violations to monitoring bodies.

13   The following codes serve as a model: ICC Charter; Code of Canadian Electricity Association; other businesses.

14   Usually applies standards of international lending agencies, otherwise uses Canadian or local standards, depending on the circumstances.

15   Company respects core labour norms set out in international treaties adhered to by Canada in all its operations.

16   Company operates in many regions.

17   Company applies US standards or greater.

18   Code applies only to company's direct operations in these regions.

19   Company operates in all regions.

20   Company attempts to exceed minimum standards and operate responsibly in all jurisdictions.

21   Company conducts analysis in each instance and decides whether to employ company, local, or World Bank standards.

22   Company has standards that "broadly" deal with this issue.

23   Company has an annual compliance certification process.

24   Company meets minimum standards and seeks to ensure that its practices do not have adverse effects on the environment or health.

25   Company answered "yes" to this question but indicated that these rights were not mentioned explicitly in the code, as the emphasis was on freedom of association.

* Manufacturing

Table 6

Detailed Breakdown of Responses to the Questionnaire by Companies with Code

		Mining Corporations							Consumer Products				Utilities		Hi-Tech			M*	Oil & Gas			
		Alcan	Aur	Cambior	Cameco	Gibraltar	Inco	Placer Dome	Dominion Textile	Dylex	Hudson's Bay	Mark's Work Wearhouse	Ontario Hydro	Hydro-Québec	Apple	Mitel	Spar Aerospace	Pratt & Whitney	Alberta Energy	Canadian Occidental	Petro-Canada	TransCanada Pipelines
Overseas Operations	South Asia	y							y		y	y	y		16		19		y	y		
	East/Central Asia	y			y						y	y	y						y			
	South-East Asia	y					y		y		y		y			y		y				
	Caribbean	y		y				y											y			
	Africa	y							y		y		y	y		y	y	y	y	y	y	y
	Eastern Europe											y				y	y	y				
	South/Central America	y	y	y	y	y	y	y	y	y	y		y		y	y	y	y	y			y
Code Applies to these Regions?		y	y	y	y	y	y	y	y	y	6	y	10	13	y	18	y	y	y	y	y	y
Code Model?		y	n		n	n	n	n	c	c	n	n	n	14		n	y		n	n	n	n
Canadian (c) or Host (h) Standards?		h	1	c	c	c	c	4	c	c	7	8	11	14	17	h	h	h	20	24	20	21
Content of the Code of Conduct	Relations with Canadian government	y	y	y	y	y	y	y	y		y		y	y	y	y	y		y	y		y
	Relations with foreign governments	y	y	y	y	y	y	y			y		y	y	y	y			y	y	y	y
	Lobbying and political contributions	y	y	y			y	y	y	y	y		y	y	y	y				y	y	y
	Bribery and kickbacks	y	y	y	y	y	y	y	y	y	y		y	y	y	y			y	y	y	y
	Operations in countries with repressive regimes			y	y		y				y		y									22
	Customer relations	y				y	y	y	y	y	y	y	y		y	y	y		y	y	y	y

Table 6 (continued)

Detailed Breakdown of Responses to the
Questionnaire by Companies with Code

	Mining Corporations							Consumer Products				Utilities		Hi-Tech			M*	Oil & Gas			
	Alcan	Aur	Cambior	Cameco	Gibraltar	Inco	Placer Dome	Dominion Textile	Dylex	Hudson's Bay	Mark's Work Wearhouse	Ontario Hydro	Hydro-Québec	Apple	Mitel	Spar Aerospace	Pratt & Whitney	Alberta Energy	Canadian Occidental	Petro-Canada	TransCanada Pipelines
Content of the Code of Conduct																					
Supplier relations	Y	Y	Y		Y	Y	Y	Y	Y	Y	Y	Y		Y	Y	Y		Y		Y	Y
Relations with employees in Canada	Y	Y	Y	Y		Y			Y	Y		Y			Y	Y		Y	Y		Y
Relations with employees abroad	Y	Y	Y	Y		Y			Y	Y		Y			Y	Y		Y	Y		Y
Worker health & safety	Y	Y	Y	Y	Y	Y		Y	Y	Y		Y		Y	Y			Y	Y	Y	Y
Worker unionization	Y		Y			Y			Y	Y					Y					Y	
Relations with investors	Y	Y	Y			Y	Y		Y	Y	Y	Y		Y	Y					Y	Y
Relations with communities	Y	Y	Y			Y		Y	Y	Y	Y	Y			Y			Y	Y	Y	Y
Environmental protection	Y	Y		Y	Y	Y			Y	Y		Y		Y	Y			Y	Y	Y	Y
Product safety	Y		Y			Y			Y	Y	Y	Y			Y		Y		Y		Y
Product quality			Y			Y			Y		Y	Y			Y			Y			
Core Labour Rights																					
Freedom of Association	Y	Y	Y	2		Y			Y		9	Y	15								
Right to organize & bargain collectively	Y		Y			Y			Y		9	25	15	Y	Y					Y	
Prohibition on forced labour	Y		Y			Y					9	Y	15								
Elimination of child labour exploitation	Y		Y			Y			Y	Y	Y	Y	15								
Non-discrimination in employment	Y	Y	Y			Y			Y		9	Y	15	Y	Y		Y			Y	Y

51

Table 6 (continued)

Detailed Breakdown of Responses to the Questionnaire by Companies with Code

		Mining Corporations							Consumer Products				Utilities		Hi-Tech			M*	Oil & Gas			
		Alcan	Aur	Cambior	Cameco	Gibraltar	Inco	Placer Dome	Dominion Textile	Dylex	Hudson's Bay	Mark's Work Wearhouse	Ontario Hydro	Hydro-Québec	Apple	Mitel	Spar Aerospace	Pratt & Whitney	Alberta Energy	Canadian Occidental	Petro-Canada	TransCanada Pipelines
Monitoring	Internal audits	y		y	y		3	y	y	y	y		y	y	y			y	y	y	y	y
	Independent audits		y	y	y	y	y				y			y	y			y				
	Supervisor surveillance	y	y	y	y	y					y	y		y	y	y	y		y		y	
	Internal committee			y							y		12	y	y	y	y	y	y	y		23
	Corporate legal counsel	y	y	y	y	n	n	y	y	5	y	y	y	y	y		y	y	y	y	y	y
Ethics reports?		n	n	y	n	n	n	n	n	n	n	y	y	y		y	n	y	n	n	n	n
Employee training?		y	n	y	n	n	n	n	y	n	y	y	y	y	y	n	n	y	n	y	y	y
Whistleblower protection?		y	n	y	n	n	y	n	y	y	y	y	y		y	y	n	y	n	n	y	y
Business has a role in human rights protection and sustainable development?		y	y		y	y	y	y	y	y	y	y	y	y	y	y	y		y	y		y

Table 7

Comparison of Questionnaire Responses and Content of Codes
(Companies that submitted both a questionnaire and a code)
q= questionnaire c= code

Corporations (Where responses are in the form of number, please see notes, page 49)

	Apple		Hydro-Québec		Hudson's Bay		Inco		Ontario Hydro		Petro-Canada		Pratt & Whitney		Spar Aerospace	
	q	c	q	c	q	c	q	c	q	c	q	c	q	c	q	c
Codes Applies Overseas?	y		y		y		y		y	y	y	y	y	y	y	
Code Model?			13		6		n		10		n				y	
Canadian (c) or Host (h) Standards?	17		14		7		c		11	y	c		h		h	
Relations with Canadian governments	y	y			y		y	y	y	y	y				y	
Relations with foreign governments	y	y			y		y		y	y					y	
Lobbying and political contributions	y	y			y		y		y		y	y		y	y	
Bribery and kickbacks	y	y	y	y	y	y	y		y	y	y	y		y	y	
Operations in countries with repressive regimes					y		y		y	y	y					
Customer relations	y	y			y		y		y		y	y		y		
Supplier relations	y				y	y	y		y	y	y	y		y		
Relations with employees in Canada			y	y	y	y	y	y	y	y		y				y
Relations with employees abroad					y	y	y		y	y	y			y		
Worker health & safety	y	y	y	y	y		y	y	y	y	y	y		y		
Worker unionization					y		y		y							
Relations with investors	y	y			y		y	y	y	y	y	y		y		y
Relations with communities					y		y		y	y	y	y				y

53

Table 7 (continued)

Comparison of Questionnaire Responses and Content of Codes
(Companies that submitted both a questionnaire and a code)

q= questionnaire   c= code

Corporations (Where responses are in the form of number, please see notes, page 49)

		Apple		Hydro-Québec		Hudson's Bay		Inco		Ontario Hydro		Petro-Canada		Pratt & Whitney		Spar Aerospace	
		q	c	q	c	q	c	q	c	q	c	q	c	q	c	q	c
Content of the Code of Conduct	Environmental protection	y	y		y	y		y	y	y	y	y	y		y		y
	Product safety					y		y	y	y			y		y		
	Product quality		y			y		y	y	y	y				y		
Core Labour Rights	Freedom of association			15						y	y		y				
	Right to organize & bargain collectively			15				y		25	y		y		y		
	Prohibition on forced labour			15				y		y	y						
	Elimination of child labour exploitation			15			y	y		y	y						
	Non-discrimination in employment	y	y	15	y	y	y	y		y	y	y	y	y	y		
Monitoring	Internal audits	y		y		y		3		y		y	y	y	y		y
	Independent audits	y		y		y		y			y	y	y	y			
	Supervisor surveillance	y	y	y		y					y	y	y			y	y
	Internal committee	y	y	y	y				y				y	y	y	y	
	Corporate legal counsel	y	y	y		y		y		y		y	y	y	y	y	
Ethics Reports?				y		n		n		y	y	n		y	y	n	
Employee Training?		y		y		y		n		12	y	y		y		n	
Whistleblower protection?		y	y			y		y		y		y	y	y	y	n	

Table 8

Responses to Telephone Survey (Companies who did not return questionnaires and companies who returned questionnaires but have no codes)

Company Name	Sector	Information from Telephone Interview			Reason for Not Returning Questionnaire	
		No Code	Has Code	Code Under Review	Reason	No Response and No Reason Given
3M Canada	Consumer Products				Recipient of too many surveys	
Banister Foundation	Manufacturing	Junior partner in joint ventures; follows overseas company lead; works with overseas unions				
Barrick Gold	Gold Mining					✓
BC Hydro	Utility					✓
Beamscope	Wholesaler					✓
Bema Gold	Gold Mining					✓
Bombardier	Manufacturing				No time	
Breakwater Resources	Gold Mining	Applies Canadian standards in overseas operations, but no written policies			No time	
Caledonian Mining	Gold Mining	Operations abide by local laws			Policy not available to public	
Caminco	Gold Mining		Code deals with business practices and includes statement on non-discrimination			
Campbell Resources	Gold Mining				Company policy not to participate in surveys	
Canadian Pacific	Conglomerate		Code deals with business practices, non-discrimination and environmental standards			
Canadian Tire	Speciality Store					✓
Cascades	Forestry					✓
Chai-Na-Ta	Manufacturing					✓

Table 8 (continued)

(Companies who did not return questionnaires and companies who returned questionnaires but have no codes)

Responses to Telephone Survey

Company Name	Sector	Information from Telephone Interview			Reason for Not Returning Questionnaire	
		No Code	Has Code	Code Under Review	Reason	No Response and No Reason Given
Consoltex	Household			Code under review		
Cornucopia	Gold Mining	Code not necessary				
Deran Industries	Manufacturing					✓
Denison Mines	Metal Mining				Survey deemed not relevant to their work	
Digital	Hi-Tech					✓
Echo Bay Mines	Gold Mining	No code			Operations overseas only exploration	
Empire Clothing	Retail					✓
Estée Lauder	Consumer Products					✓
Falconbridge	Integrated Mining	No code; maintains Canadian standards in overseas operations; believes business has a role to play in human rights protection and sustainable development		Working with Mining Association of Canada to develop code		
Finning	Wholesaler					✓
Four Seasons Hotel	Services					✓
Franco Nevada	Gold Mining					✓
General Electric	Manufacturing					✓
Gibraltar	Metals Mining					✓
Golden Star Resources	Gold Mining				No time	
Gulf Canada	Oil				Has a distant relationship with its overseas operations in Indonesia and unsure how they operate	

Table 8 (continued)

(Companies who did not return questionnaires and companies who returned questionnaires but have no codes)

Responses to Telephone Survey		Information from Telephone Interview			Reason for Not Returning Questionnaire	
Company Name	Sector	No Code	Has Code	Code Under Review	Reason	No Response and No Reason Given
Hartco. Entreprises	Speciality Stores					✓
Hemlo Gold Mines	Gold Mining				No time	
Hewlett Packard	Hi-Tech		Code deals with business practices; no labour standards; no environmental standards			
IBM	Hi-Tech				No time, operate mostly in Canada	
Inmet Mining	Integrated Mining					✓
Irwin Toy	Household					✓
Jean Coutu	Speciality Stores					✓
K-Mart	Retail					✓
Kaufel Group	Manufacturing	No code; follow local host country studies			Code not a priority area	
Kinross Gold	Gold Mining					✓
Le Château	Retail					✓
Linamar Corporation	Manufacturing				Decline to participate, survey n/a	
Loblaws	Food					✓
MacMillan Bloedel	Forestry					✓
Magna International	Automotive		Employee "charter" includes reference to health and safety; wages; fair treatment; anonymous complaints mechanism			
Methanex	Chemical					✓

Table 8 (continued)

(Companies who did not return questionnaires and companies who returned questionnaires but have no codes)

Responses to Telephone Survey

Company Name	Sector	Information from Telephone Interview			Reason for Not Returning Questionnaire	
		No Code	Has Code	Code Under Review	Reason	No Response and No Reason Given
Minera Rayrock	Metals Mining	Maintains North American standards in all operations			No time	
Miramar	Metals Mining				No time	
Moore Company	Manufacturing				No time	
Newbridge	Hi-Tech			Work on code in progress		
Norcen Energy	Oil				No time	
Northgate	Gold Mining				Sold international operations (Chile)	
Pan Canadian Petroleum	Oil			Reviewing code		
Pantorama	Retail					✓
Peerless Carpet	Household					✓
Pegasus Gold	Gold Mining		Statement of policy regarding environmental protection; environmental protection considered in evaluating employee performance			
Pharma Plus	Specialty Stores	Too difficult to evaluate activities of suppliers; relies on government guidance; hopes neutral body can do evaluation				
Price/Costco	Retail					✓
Proctor & Gamble	Consumer Products					✓
Provigo	Food		Code deals with business practices and labour standards such as non-discrimination and health and safety; is not a supplier code			

Table 8 (continued)

(Companies who did not return questionnaires and companies who returned questionnaires but have no codes)

Responses to Telephone Survey		Information from Telephone Interview			Reason for Not Returning Questionnaire	
Company Name	Sector	No Code	Has Code	Code Under Review	Reason	No Response and No Reason Given
Rea Gold	Gold Mining					✓
Reitmans	Retail	Too difficult to evaluate activities of suppliers, though agrees with idea in principle				
Rio Algom	Metals Mining				No time	
Sears Canada	Retail					✓
Semi-Tech	Household				Not part of the holding company's responsibilities	
Shaw Industries	Manufacturing				Selective about surveys will respond to; codes of conduct survey not a priority	
SHL Systemhouse	Hi-Tech					✓
SNC Lavalin	Services			Reviewing code		
Sodisco-Hawden	Speciality Stores					
Susy Shier	Retail				No time	✓
Teck Corporation	Gold Mining				No time	
TVX Gold	Gold Mining	Follows host national standards as a minimum and has policy on worker health and safety				
Vengold	Gold Mining	No code; maintains Canadian standards in all operations; uses supervisor surveillance to monitor; believes business has a role to play in human rights protection and sustainable development				
Viceroy Resources	Gold Mining					✓
Xerox	Hi-Tech					✓
Zellers	Retail				Unable to do survey because of restructuring	

NOTES

Please note that footnotes are ordered as follows:

> Author, "Title of article," volume number *title of publication*
> issue number (date), page number.

1   See Edward Gargan, "Business Objects to a Code in China," *New York Times* (May 24, 1994), p. D2; Steven Mufson, "For US Firms, a Struggle over Rights and Roles," *Washington Post* (August 25, 1994), p. B10; David Sanger, "Clinton to urge a Rights Code for Businesses Dealing Abroad," *New York Times* (March 27, 1995), p. D1; Clay Chandler, "Code of Conduct: Draft Assailed: Rights Groups Criticize Administration's Rules for US Firms Abroad," *New York Times* (March 28, 1995), p. D4.; A.M. Rosenthal, "The Limp Noodle," *New York Times* (March 28, 1995), p. A19; Steven Mufson, "The Beijing Duck: What US Firms in China Don't Do for Human Rights," *New York Times* (April 9, 1995), p. C1.

Very generally worded and extremely brief, the Principles encourage corporations to implement codes of conduct that deal with worker health and safety, fair employment practices, environmental protection, compliance with laws and an ethical corporate culture. The Principles lack any form of regular reporting mechanisms. Corporations are merely urged to publicize their actions. According to the Commerce Department brief on the Principles, the Clinton Administration aims to promote its model code by supporting conferences, sharing the code with other nations, and placing the code on the agenda during meetings between the President and US business leaders. At the same time, the Principles were issued on paper not bearing the imprint of the White House, suggesting that Presidential support for the initiative is lukewarm (Richard Dicker, Human Rights Watch, statement to NGO Round Table on Social Responsibility of Canadian Business Abroad, University of Ottawa, May 23, 1996). Further, little seems to have been done since March 1995 to promote the Principles. The responsible officials at the Department of Commerce are no longer with the agency and no one seems to have taken up their task (Department of Commerce, Personal Communication, August 12, 1996). Other analysts have made similar observations. See for example, Douglass Cassel, "Corporate Initiatives: A Second Human Rights Revolution," 19 *Fordham International Law Journal* (1996), p. 1975. "No one in Washington seems to be monitoring how many firms have actually taken up the invitation to adopt codes reflecting the Model Principles... By March 1996, the Commerce Department's efforts appear to consist mainly of looking for a place to put an information clearinghouse, and working on nomination procedures for the awards it plans to hand out annually to firms exemplifying the Model Principles." Presently, San Francisco-based Business for Social Responsibility is to serve as a clearinghouse for codes of conduct. By June 1995, only one company — Honeywell — had rewritten "its own code to address human rights issues included in the president's model business principles.": Rita Beamish, "Businesses Slow to Embrace Clinton's Code of Conduct," *Associated Press* (June 18, 1995).

2   In 1991, a congressional bill was introduced by US Representative John Miller (R-WA) and set out standards of behaviour for US corporations operating in China and Tibet. Known popularly as the Miller Principles, the code includes a ban on US corporate involvement with goods produced by China's extensive prison labour system, occupational health and safety features and recognition of rights of association for workers. See The Miller Principles, reprinted in H.R. 1571, 102d Congress, 1st Sess. (1991). Corporations engaged in economic cooperation projects in China or Tibet would be required to register with the Secretary of State six months following the bill's enactment. The corporation would then be asked whether it agrees to abide by the Principles. Corporations agreeing to the code would file annual reports on their performance. The Secretary of State would also be asked to produce annual reports on corporate performance and submit these to Congress and the OECD. US government agencies dealing with export marketing would intercede only on behalf of corporations adhering to the Principles. While the Miller Principles were not signed into law, they have been reintroduced in subsequent sessions of Congress, including the recent 104th Congress. See H.R. 1147, I.H. 104th Congress 1st Sess. (1995). The Miller Principles passed the House of Representatives as part of the Omnibus Export Amendment Act of 1991 in October 1991 and then were referred to a joint House-Senate conference. Subsequently, a conference bill passed the Senate on October 8, 1992, was not voted upon in the House for reasons unrelated to the Principles themselves.

Another bill introduced in the last session of the US House of Representatives would require the Secretary of State to establish a set of voluntary guidelines to promote socially responsible business practices for US businesses operating in foreign countries. See H.R. 910, I.H. 104th Congress 1st Sess. (1995). The bill required several government and non-governmental bodies to collaborate in developing a code of conduct for US businesses operating overseas by drawing on existing codes, including the Miller, MacBride and Sullivan Principles. US businesses operating overseas would report to the Secretary of State on their observance of this code. As with earlier bills relating to the MacBride Principles, the Miller Principles and the Sullivan Principles, the bill indicated that "[d]epartments and agencies of the United States may intercede with a foreign government or foreign national regarding export marketing activity in a foreign country on behalf of a United States national ... only if that United States national complies with the guidelines."

3   See Parliament of Canada, Standing Committee on Sustainable Human Development of the House of Commons, *Minutes of Proceedings and Evidence* (October 2, 1996).

4   See discussion in L. Compa and T. Hinchcliffe-Darricarrère, "Enforcing International Labor Rights through Corporate Codes of Conduct," 33 *Columbia Journal of Transnational Law* (1995), p. 674.

5   Al Cook, CLAIHR Coordinator, (former Deputy Director of the International Defence and Aid Fund for South Africa, former Executive Director of Canada-South Africa Cooperation), statement to NGO Round Table on Social Responsibility of Canadian Business Abroad, University of Ottawa, May 23, 1996. See also Daniel Pink, "The Valdez Principles: Is What's Good for America Good for General Motors?" 8 *Yale Law and Public Review* (1990), p. 180

6   Al Cook, *supra* note 5.

7   Officer of Consumer Affairs, "Voluntary Codes and the Consumer Interest," 1 *Consumer Quarterly* 4 (October 1996), p. 2.

8   Ross Cranston, *Consumers and the Law* (London: Weidenfeld & Nicholson, 1978). See summary in Lola Fabowalé, *Voluntary Codes: A Viable Alternative to Government Legislation?* (Ottawa: Public Interest Advocacy Centre, 1994).

9   See Robert Sweeney and Howard Siers, "Ethics in Corporate America," 71 *Management Accounting* 12 (June 1990), p. 34. (56% of US corporations have codes); "Survey Examines Corporate Ethics Policies," 173 *Journal of Accountancy* 2 (Feb. 1988), p. 16. (75% of large US corporations have codes).

10   See Ethics Resource Center, *Creating a Workable Company Code of Ethics* (Washington, 1990). See also, Frank Bradley, "Prepare to Make a Moral Judgement," *People Management* (May 4, 1995).

11   Len Brooks, *Canadian Corporate Social Performance* (Hamilton: Society of Management Accountants, 1986), p. 75.

12   H. Schroeder, *Report to Survey Participants on Corporate Social Performance in Canada: A Survey* (Lethbridge: School of Management, University of Lethbridge March, 1983).

13   The authors concluded that the bulk of firms who failed to respond to their enquiry did not have any codes.

14   Maurica Lefebvre and Jang Singh, "The Content and Focus of Canadian Corporate Codes of Ethics," 11 *Journal of Business Ethics* (1992), p. 799.

15   Id.; Findings on ethical behaviour in the UK demonstrate that corporate social responsibility outside of the firm also ranks low on business priorities in Britain. See John Humble, David Jackson and Alan Thomson, "The Strategic Power of Corporate Values," 27 *Long Range Planning* (1994), p. 28: "[a] survey in the UK shows that 80 per cent of organizations have written statements of values, the most important being people, competitiveness, customers and productivity. The lowest ranked were social responsibility and profitability."

16   See Messod Beniesh and Robert Chatov, "Corporate Codes of Conduct: Economic Determinants and Legal Implications for Independent Auditors," 12 *Journal of Accounting and Public Policies* (1993), p. 5: "[W]e find that rational managers choose content [in codes] so as to reduce the expected cost of adverse legal or regulatory action conditional on firms' structure and visibility."

17   Cecily Raiborn and Dinah Payne, "Corporate Codes of Conduct: A Collective Conscience and Continuum," 9 *Journal of Business Ethics* (1990), p. 881.

18   Id.

19   Bradley, *supra* note 10. See Jeffrey Kaplan and Willian Perry, "The High Cost of Corporate Crime: How Firms Can Protect Themselves From Potential Huge Liabilities," *Management Accounting* (Dec. 1991).

20   Lefebvre and Singh, *supra* note 14, p. 808.

21   Clarkson Centre for Business Ethics, University of Toronto, written personal communication, July 1996.

22   Robert Ford and Woodrow Richardson, "Ethical Decision Making and Empirical Literature," 13 *Journal of Business Ethics* (1994), p. 216.

23   Id.

24   Raiborn and Payner, *supra* note 17, p. 884.

25   See Bradley, *supra* note 10. See also Michael Lane, "Improving American Business Ethics in Three Steps," *CPA Journal* (Feb 1991).

26   See discussion in Bradley, *supra* note 10.

27   See summary in Beniesh and Chatov, *supra* note 16, p. 6.

28   Anne Rich, Carl Smith and Paul Mihalek, "Are Corporate Codes of Conduct Effective?" *Management Accounting* (Sept. 1990). Perhaps the most notorious recent example of highly unethical behaviour by a firm with a well-respected code of conduct is that of Dow Corning. While Dow Corning possessed a code of ethics that was widely acclaimed and touted by observers as precedent setting (to such an extent that it was used in business school ethics courses), its behaviour over the course of its long involvement with breast implants fell well short of the standards set out in its code. See John Byrne, *Informed Consent: A Story of Personal Tragedy and Corporate Betrayal Inside the Silicone Breast Implant Crisis* (New York: McGraw-Hill, 1996).

29   These codes were as follows: *A Code of Practice in the Financial Sector; The Canadian Association of Broadcasters' Code on Television Violence; Canadian Bankers Association Model Privacy Code; The Canadian Bar Association Code of Ethics; The Canadian Cable Television Customer Service Standards; The Canadian Code of Practice for Debit Card Services; The Canadian Direct Marketing Association Code of Ethics; The Canadian Medical Association Code of Ethics; The Canadian Real Estate Association Code of Ethics; The Department of Communications Six Privacy Principles; Stentor Code of Fair Information Practices and Derivative Codes of Provincial Telephone Companies*, and; *Principles and Guidelines for Environmental Labelling and Advertising.*

30   Fabowalé, *supra* note 8.

31   Id., p. 16.

32   Ron Fournier, "Continued Liquor Ad Ban Urged," *Associated Press* (June 16, 1996).

33   Dennis Bueckert, "Cigarette Manufacturers Violate Own Ethics, Will Rewrite Code," *Canadian Press* (June 5, 1996).

34   Marina Strauss, "Baby Formula Industry Reneges on Code," *Globe and Mail* (July 12, 1996), p. 33.

35   Allan McChesney, *Promoting Public Interest Goals Through Business Codes of Conduct: Lessons from National (Domestic) Experience* (unpublished report prepared for CLAIHR, 1996). See also Allan McChesney (with contributions from Mark Haney), *Consumer Interest Test: Twelve Principles for Assessing Regulatory Alternatives* (Ottawa: Consumers Association of Canada, 1994). See also Office of Consumer Affairs, Industry Canada, *Summary of the Symposium on Voluntary Codes*, Ottawa, Sept. 12-13, 1996; Office of Consumer Affairs, *supra* note 7.

36   Some analysts attribute much of the success of the "Responsible Care" initiative of the Canadian chemical manufacturers to this factor. See Allan McChesney, *Responsible Care Initiative: Canadian Chemical Producers Association* (Ottawa: OECD and Treasury Board of Canada, 1994).

37   See Ann Rowan, *Statutory Recognition of Industry Codes of Ethics: A Discussion Paper* (Toronto: Ministry of Consumer and Commercial Relations, 1988).

38   Id.; Carmen Baggaley, *Voluntary Codes: Do They Have a Future?* (Comments to the Consumer and Corporate Affairs, Canada, Price Waterhouse, Symposium on Voluntary Codes, 1991); David McKendry and Carman Baggaley, *Privacy Principles Implementation Models* (Ottawa: Department of Communications, 1992).

39   Sweeney and Siers, *supra* note 9.

40   Raiborn and Payner, *supra* note 17, p. 884.

41   Lefebvre and Singh, *supra* note 14, p. 807.

42   OECD, *Trade and Labour Standards*, COM/DEELSA/TD (1995), p. 5.

43   A key element of international labour rights, freedom of association, is protected by International Labour Organization Conventions No. 87 (1948) and No. 98 (1949). The Universal Declaration of Human Rights, art. 20, also deals with rights of association and protects the right to form and to join trade unions for the protection of one's interests in Article 23. The International Covenant on Civil and Political Rights defines a right to "freedom of association with others, including the right to form and join trade unions for the protection of one's interests" in Article 22. See also Article 8 of the International Covenant on Economic, Social and Cultural Rights.

44   The right to non-discrimination permeates international legal instruments . See for example, International Covenant on Economic, Social and Cultural Rights, art. 7: Countries are to ensure that workers enjoy "equal opportunity for everyone to be promoted in his employment to an appropriate higher level, subject to no considerations other than those of seniority and competence." See also ILO 1949 Recommendation Concerning Labour Clauses in Public Contracts and ILO 111 (Discrimination, Employment and Occupation Convention, 1958).

45   Sexual orientation is not explicitly included in international bans on discrimination. However, in 1994 the United Nations Human Rights Committee ruled in a challenge brought against a Tasmanian law that the ban on discrimination on the basis of "sex" found in the UN Covenant on Civil and Political Rights also includes a ban on discrimination for reason of "sexual

orientation." See (Commun. No. 488/1992) (31 Mar. 1994) (50th Session), UN HR Committee Doc. No. CCPR/C/50/D/488/1992, 1 I.H.R.R. 96. See discussion in R. Wintemute, *Sexual Orientation and Human Rights* (Oxford: Clarendon Press, 1995), p. 148. Canadian tribunals, when asked to interpret a similar absence in Canadian human rights laws, have "read in" discrimination on the basis of sexual orientation as a prohibited grounds. See *Haig v. Canada* (1992), 9 O.R. (3d) 495, 16 C.H.R.R. D/226 (Ont. C.A.); *Vriend v. Alberta*, [1994] C.R.D. 350 (Alberta Q.B.).

46   Between 1919 and 1973, a large number of ILO conventions dealing with the minimum age of employment were introduced. In this regard, ILO 7 (1920) introduced a minimum age requirement of 14 for maritime work. ILO 15 (1921) placed the age floor at 18 for maritime employees operating as trimmers or stokers. ILO 10 (1921) sets down a minimum age of 14 for agricultural work, subject to the caveat that younger children may work so long as this does not detract from their schooling. ILO 33 (1931) introduces a standard of 14 years for non-industrial, non-agricultural employment. In 1936 and 1937, ILO 58, 59 and 60 raised the minimum age in the industrial, maritime and non-industrial sectors to 15. ILO 123 (1965) sets a minimum age of 16 for mine work. In 1973, these instruments were consolidated into a single convention, ILO 138. The treaty commits ratifying states to pursue policies consistent with the abolition of child labour and the progressive raising of the national minimum employment age to a level conducive to the full physical and mental development of children. Minimum ages are to be set with reference to the age of completion of compulsory schooling and should not be lower than 15 in developed countries and 14 in developing nations. Higher age floors are to exist in job areas which might have harmful health, safety or moral effects on young people. Other international instruments outside of those introduced by the ILO have also addressed child labour issues. See Article 10 of the International Covenant on Economic, Social and Cultural Rights. See also the UN Convention on the Rights of the Child.

47   The ILO has pledged to adopt a new standard on the elimination of the most "intolerable forms" of child labour by 1999. Note, however, that Article 32 of the existing Convention on the Rights of the Child indicates that "states parties recognize the right of the child to be protected from economic exploitation and from performing any work that is likely to be hazardous or to interfere with the child's education, or to be harmful to the child's health or physical, mental, spiritual, moral or social development." The Convention on the Rights of the Child is among the most widely ratified treaties in history. At the present time, only 6 countries have not signed it.

48   Under the first ILO forced labour treaty, Convention 29 of 1930, forced labour is outlawed, with forced labour being defined as "all work or service which is exacted from any person under the menace of penalty and for which the said person has not offered himself voluntarily." The Universal Declaration of Human Rights and the Covenant on Civil and Political Rights provide that "no one should be held in slavery or servitude" (Article 4) and that "everyone has the right to free choice of employment" (Article 23). Further, under Article 8 of the Convention, "no one shall be required to perform forced or compulsory labour" except in certain

specific instances related to national service and imprisonment with hard labour. Similarly, Article 6 of the Convention states that the right to work includes "the right of everyone to the opportunity to gain his living by work which he freely chooses or accepts."

49   OECD, *supra* note 42.

50   Convention 29 on forced labour had 135 ratifications by 1995, Convention 98 on the rights to organize and bargain collectively had 123, Convention 100 on equal pay 120, Convention 111 on non-discrimination 118, Convention 11 on rights of association in agriculture 114, Conventions 14 and 19 on weekly rest in industry 113, Convention 105 on forced labour 112, Convention 81 on labour inspection 111, Convention 87 on freedom of association 109, and Convention 138 on child labour 46.

51   19 U.S.C., paragraph 2702(b)(7).

52   See International Labour Convention No. 155 (Occupational Safety and Health and the Working Environment, 1981); International Covenant on Economic, Social and Cultural Rights, art. 7.

53   See ILO Convention 131 (Concerning Minimum Wage Fixing, with Special Reference to Developing Countries). Article 3 indicates that in setting minimum wages, countries should consider the needs of workers and their families as assessed with reference to the general level of wages in the country, the cost of living, social security benefits and the relative standards of living of other social groups. Countries should also consider economic factors such as economic development and desirability of maintaining high employment. ILO Recommendation 135 (1970) is also of relevance. This document indicates that "[i]n determining the level of minimum wages, account should be taken of the following criteria, amongst others: (a) the needs of workers and their families; (b) the general level of wages in the country; (c) the cost of living and changes therein; (d) social security benefits; (e) economic factors, including the requirements of economic development, levels of productivity and the desirability of attaining and maintaining a high level of employment. See also the Universal Declaration of Human Rights, art. 23(3) and Article 7 of the International Covenant on Economic, Social, and Cultural Rights.

54   A number of ILO Conventions deal with working hours, ILO Convention No. 1 limits normal working hours to eight per day and no more than 48 per week. Convention No. 14 (1921) indicates that workers should generally have a least one 24 hour period of rest each week. See also the Universal Declaration of Human Rights, Article 24: "Everyone has the right to rest and leisure, including reasonable limitation of working hours and periodic holidays with pay." Likewise, the International Covenant on Economic, Social and Cultural Rights provides in Article 7 that countries will ensure that workers enjoy "rest, leisure and reasonable limitation of working hours and periodic holidays with pay, as well as remuneration for public holidays."

55   See Douglass Cassel, *supra* note 1, p. 1974. The Business for Social Responsibility survey apparently focussed on businesses selected for their significance and

the surveyor's sense that they would be likely to have codes (ie. labour intensive textile firms, retailers). Aaron Cramer, Director, Business and Human Rights Program, Business for Social Responsibility Education Fund, personal communication, August 1996.

56   The Franklin pollsters focussed on major US retailers and brand name goods manufacturers. Simon Billenness, Franklin Research and Development, personal communication, February 1997.

57   US Department of Labor, *The Apparel Industry and Codes of Conduct: A Solution to the International Child Labour Problem?* (1996). The Department of Labor survey focussed on the largest apparel manufacturers, department stores and mass merchandisers as measured by 1995 annual sales figures.

58   Id. p. 26.

59   See L. Compa *et al, supra* note 4, p. 676, summarizing the Levi Strauss & Co., *Sourcing Guidelines Working Group Report to Executive Management Committee* (1993).

60   Id.

61   Levi's, Id.

62   See Compa *et al, supra* note 4, p. 679; John McCormick and Marc Levinson, "The Supply Police," *Newsweek* (February 15, 1993), p. 48. In one instance described by Compa, *supra*, Levi's worked with its Bangladeshi suppliers employing children under 14 to pay the children wages to go back to school. Subsequently, the children will be reinstated at the factories when they turn 14. This model was extended to other non-Levi's Bangladeshi factories recently after the US threatened Bangladesh with trade measures.

63   Vivian Marino, "Garment Workers Get Attention," *Associated Press* (June 18, 1996).

64   D. Orentlicher and T. Gelatt, "Public Law, Private Actors: The Impact of Human Rights on Business Investors in China," 14 *Northwestern Journal of International Law & Business* (1993), p. 106. See also Andy Borrus and Joyce Barnathan, "Staunching the Flow of China's Gulag Exports," *Business Week* (April 12, 1992), p. 50.

65   Compa *et al, supra* note 4.

66   Joel Makower, *Beyond The Bottom Line* (New York: Simon & Schuster 1996), p. 277.

67   See Compa *et al, supra* note 4, p. 679; "Bailing Out of Burma," *New York Times Magazine* (April 2, 1995), p. 18; G. Pascal Zachary, "US Companies Back Out of Burma, Citing Human Rights Concerns, Graft," *Wall Street Journal* (April 12, 1995), p. A10. Other firms that have pulled out of Burma include Liz Claiborne, Eddie Bauer and Macy's owner, Federated Department Stores. See "Ethical Shopping: Human Rights," *The Economist* (June 3, 1995). Petro-Canada and Scotiabank also appear to have ceased dealing with Burma.

68   Orentlicher and Gelatt, *supra* note 64.

69   Id., p. 106.

70   Sears, *Code of Business Conduct*, p. 4.

71   Reebok, *Human Rights Production Standards* (1993).

72   See "Human Rights Production Standards Set in Worldwide Reebok Initiative," *Reebok: Making A Difference*, company newsletter (June 1993): "[c]onsumers today hold companies accountable for the way products are made, not just the quality of the product itself."

73   Compa *et al, supra* note 4, p. 682.

74   Id.

75   Marino, *supra* note 63.

76   None of these companies responded to repeated requests for copies of their codes of conduct. Wal-Mart refused to release its code, indicating that is was available to associates only, though it later supplied a copy to the US Department of Labor. See US Department of Labor, *supra* note 57, for copies of these and other codes.

77   "Ethical Shopping: Human Rights," *supra* note 67.

78   See Compa *et al, supra,* note 4.

79   In 1984, Congress added labour conditions on the extension and renewal of General System of Preferences tariff benefit to potentially eligible nations. An infringement of "internationally recognized worker rights" would remove a nation from eligibility under the system. US practice in recent years has been to rely to a growing extent on the standards set out in international labour conventions to measure compliance with the GSP conditions. The evidence suggests that this system has had a beneficial impact on the labour policies of US trading partners. In 1995, the European Union (EU) followed the US lead in establishing labour conditionalities for its own GSP program. Developing nations with good labour records are granted even lower tariffs than under the straight GSP. The US has also tied labour standards to its unfair trade remedy under Super 301 of the Trade Act. Section 301 envisages retaliation for trade practices deemed "unreasonable" or "inequitable." Unreasonable behaviour includes conduct that harms workers' rights as defined by the GSP conditions. For discussion see C. Forcese, "Jean Chrétien meets Oliver Twist: Using Trade Law to Address Forced Child Labour," unpublished paper available from the author (May 1996); "The Liberals' New Trade Challenge: Using Trade Law to Address Child Labour," *Amnesty International Legal Network Newsletter*, Canada (Winter 1996). See also P. Harvey, *US GSP Labour Rights Conditionality* (Washington, D.C.: International Labour Rights Fund, 1995). For the relationship between these measures and codes see Compa *et al, supra* note 3, p. 675.

80   US legislators, galvanized by the sense that foreigners are competing unfairly, have been persistent in arguing that the next rounds of trade talks will be dominated by the "blue and green" agenda: labour and environment. For its part,

the European Union hopes to devise World Trade Organization rules that would outlaw forced and child labour. See E. de Wet, "Labor Standards in the Globalized Economy: The Inclusion of a Social Clause in the General Agreement on Tariffs and Trade/World Trade Organization," 17 *Human Rights Quarterly* (1995), p. 445; "US Proposal to Bring Worker Rights Issues Up at GATT Council Draws Cautious Response," 4 *International Trade Report* (July 22, 1987), p. 942; "Worker Rights in Current GATT Negotiations," *Worker Rights News* (June 1988). See also T. Buerkle, "European Leaders Woo New Partners," *The Globe and Mail* (February 29, 1996), p. A2. For a comprehensive discussion of the linkage issue, see OECD, *supra* note 42. Christine Elwell, *Human Rights, Labour Standards and the new WTO* (Montreal: ICHRDD, 1995); Virginia Leary, "Workers' Rights and International Trade," in Bhagwati and Hudec (eds.) *Fair Trade and Harmonization* (Cambridge: MIT Press, 1996). In December 1996, the members of the WTO failed to agree on some means of enforcing labour standards via the trade regime but did commit to observance of internationally recognized labour standards. See Carolyn Henson, "Global Trade Pact Imminent," *Associated Press* (December 12, 1996).

81   See, for example, *Labor Union of Pico Korea v. Pico Products*, 968 F.2d 191 (2d Cir. 1992); *Dow Chemical Co. v. Castro-Alfaro*, 786 S.W.2d 674 (Tex. 1990).

82   For discussion, see Tim Smith, "Pressures from Above," 81 *Business and Society Review* (1992), p. 36. For reports on the activities of socially conscious institutional investors in influencing labour practices of corporations, see Franci Flaherty, "Nice Profits, Hard Ethics for Political Correctness," *New York Times* (Nov. 27, 1993), p. 33; Albert Crenshaw, "Where Responsibility Meets Accountability," *Washington Post* (Nov. 28, 1994), p. 5; Carol Gould, "A Social Responsibility Shake-Up," *New York Times* (June 12, 1994), p. 14. For a quick outline of how shareholder activism has (or might) work, see C. Forcese, *Owning Up: The Case for Making Corporate Managers More Responsive to Shareholder Values* (Ottawa: Democracy Watch, 1997). For a general overview of these issues, see Compa *et al*, *supra* note 4, p. 674- 5.

83   S. Coats, "Organizing and Oppression," 16 *Multinational Monitor* 6 (1995), p. 17.

84   Rev. David Schilling, Director, Global Corporate Accountability Program, Interfaith Center on Corporate Responsibility, at the *International Child Labor Public Hearings*, US Department of Labor, Washington DC (June 28, 1996).

85   Personal communication, January 25, 1996. See also National Labor Committee, *The US in Haiti* (1996), p. 40: "Over the years, the National Labor Committee has interviewed hundreds of *maquila* workers across the [Caribbean] region. When you ask the young women (who make up the vast majority of *maquila* workers) about these corporate codes of conduct, they do not have the slightest idea of what you are talking about. When we explained the concept, we have had women respond: 'Our code is the screwdriver and the sun. To punish us they hit us on the head with the butt of a screw driver or put us out into the blazing sun for the day, or even every day for a week.'"

86   J. Ballinger, "Just Do It — Or Else," 16 *Multinational Monitor* 6 (1995), p. 7.

87   US Department of Labor, *supra* note 57, p. 46.

88   Id. at p., vii.

89   Bob Ortega, "Conduct Codes Garner Goodwill for Retailers, But Violations Go On," *Associated Press* (July 3, 1995).

90   Compa *et al, supra* note 4, p. 686; Lauri Udesky, "Sweatshops Behind the Labels: The 'Social Responsibility' Gap," *The Nation* (May 16, 1994), p. 665.

91   ITGLWF Newsletter clipping on file with author.

92   Ortega, *supra* note 89.

93   See Compa *et al, supra* note 4, p. 686. Jessie Jackson recently condemned both Reebok and Nike for running "sweatshops" in Asia. While Reebok permitted Jackson to inspect one of its facilities, Nike refused such permission. See "Asian Workers' Rights Studied," *Globe and Mail* (July 22, 1996).

94   Ballinger, *supra* note 86. For a comprehensive critique of Nike and Levi's performance in applying their codes see *There is No Finish Line, Report of the International IRENE/AGIR ICI Workshop on Transnational Corporations* (on file with the author).

95   C. Kernaghan, personal communication, January 25, 1996.

96   Coats, *supra* note 83.

97   Paul Puritt, Canadian Labour Congress, quoted in Stephen Dale, "Teddy Bears Warn of Asian Sweatshops," *Inter-Press Service* (Nov. 30, 1995).

98   US Department of Labor, *supra* note 57, p., v.

99   Id., p. 101.

100   Id., p. 107.

101   C. Forcese, "Latin Mandarin," 16 *Multinational Monitor* 9 (1995), p. 4. See also Bob Herbert, "Not a Living Wage," *The New York Times* (Oct. 9, 1995); Bob Herbert, "In Deep Denial," *The New York Times* (Oct. 13, 1995); NLC, Press Release: "The 'Authentic Gap': How Would You Like Your Daughter to Work for The Gap?" (Nov./Dec. 1995); Bob Herbert, "A Sweatshop Victory," *The New York Times* (Dec. 22, 1995); Randolph Ryan, "The Gap Agrees to Pressure El Salvador Firm," *The Boston Globe* (Dec. 20, 1995); Gayle Lilies, "The US-Salvador Gap," 17 *Multinational Monitor* 1 (1996), p. 7.

102   See Herbert *supra* note 101; Leslie Ravan, "Christmas Jeer," *The Village Voice* (Dec. 26, 1995). In one notable instance demonstrating the anger revelations of abuse at Mandarin International caused,

> [t]wo rabbis from Congregation B'nai Jeshurun on Manhattan's Upper West Side wrote a letter to Donald G. Fisher, chief executive of The Gap and Banana Republic empire, that said, "Before we publicly announce to our congregation that shopping at The Gap and the Banana Republic is a violation of Jewish ethical laws, we would like to hear from you if there are any plans to immediately correct those violations."

103   B. Herbert, *supra* note 101.

104   C. Kernaghan, personal communication, January 25, 1996.

105   US Department of Labor, *supra* note 57, at 111.

106   ICCR, *Independent Monitoring Working Group Progress Report* (April 19, 1996).

107   Id.

108   Schilling, *supra* note 108.

109   Id.

110   The four OECD labour rights were broken into five discrete rights for the purposes of this study; freedom of association and the right to organize and bargain collectively were disaggregated. The division reflects the tendency in Canadian law — and possibly also business circles — to view the right to organize and bargain collectively as a right not encompassed by freedom of association. See *Reference Re Public Service Relations Act (Alta.)* 1987, 87 C.L.L.C. 189 (S.C.C.).

111   See discussion in Lefebvre and Singh, *supra* note 14, p. 801: "It is assumed that a large majority of the ... companies which did not respond to the ... [survey] do not have established corporate codes of ethics. In view of the current escalating trend towards ethics, it is presumed that an organization which had developed ethical policy statements would have readily submitted the document, for this would enhance the company's image by affirming its commitment to operating in an ethical manner."

112   Table 5 also includes data from codes of conduct when these were supplied along with the questionnaire. In some instances, the respondent clearly meant us to use the supplied code to fill out many of the code content questions.

113   See Desiree Kissoon Jodah, "Courting Disaster in Guyana," 16 *Multinational Monitor* 10 (Nov. 1995).

114   See Associated Press, "Philippines Revokes Mine Permit: Action Follows Pollution by Copper Mining Company in Which Placer Dome has Stake," *Globe and Mail* (June 25, 1996), p. B8.

115   US Department of Labor, *supra* note 57, p. 113.

116   Id.

About CLAIHR

The Canadian Lawyers Association for International Human Rights (CLAIHR) is a non-profit, non-governmental organization, established to promote and protect human rights internationally through the use of law and legal institutions.

CLAIHR :
- analyses laws, institutions and practices affecting human rights;
- contributes to developing and strengthening laws and institutions that protect human rights;
- promotes awareness of human rights issues within the legal community;
- supports lawyers, legal organizations and others dedicated to achieving human rights.

CLAIHR puts Canadian lawyers' experience and expertise to work to further civil, political, economic, social and cultural rights worldwide. CLAIHR can be reached at:
204-251 Laurier Ave. West, Ottawa, Ontario K1P 5J6 Canada
Tel: (613) 233-0398;   Fax: (613) 233-0671; E-mail: claihr@web.net

About ICHRDD

The International Centre for Human Rights and Democratic Development (ICHRDD) was established (by an Act of the Parliament of Canada) in 1988. Its mandate is to defend and promote the rights and freedoms enshrined in the International Bill of Rights and encourage the development of democratic societies. The Centre promotes the principle of universality of human rights and places equal emphasis on social, economic, cultural, civil and political rights. The Centre provides financial, political and technical support to front-line organizations in developing countries in order to help establish effective human rights institutions and practices, and encourage the development of democratic civil societies. The Centre also plays an advocacy and educational role both in Canada and abroad, speaking out about human rights abuses and advocating policies to reduce their incidence. ICHRDD can be reached at:
63, rue de Brésoles, Montreal, Quebec H2Y 1V7 Canada
Tel: (514) 283-6073; Fax: (514) 283-3792; E-mail: ichrdd@web.net
You may also visit our web page at http://www. ichrdd.ca